better than new

better than new

Tips for Upcycling and Refinishing Furniture

chloe kempster

HERBERT PRESS
LONDON · OXFORD · NEW YORK · NEW DELHI · SYDNEY

HERBERT PRESS
Bloomsbury Publishing Plc
50 Bedford Square, London, WC1B 3DP, UK
29 Earlsfort Terrace, Dublin 2, Ireland

BLOOMSBURY, HERBERT PRESS and the Herbert Press logo are trademarks of Bloomsbury Publishing Plc

First published in Great Britain in 2024

Copyright © Chloe Kempster 2024

Chloe Kempster has asserted her rights under the Copyright, Designs and Patents Act, 1988, to be identified as Author of this work

All rights reserved. No part of this publication may be reproduced or transmitted in any form or by any means, electronic or mechanical, including photocopying, recording, or any information storage or retrieval system, without prior permission in writing from the publishers

Bloomsbury Publishing Plc does not have any control over, or responsibility for, any third-party websites referred to or in this book. All internet addresses given in this book were correct at the time of going to press. The author and publisher regret any inconvenience caused if addresses have changed or sites have ceased to exist, but can accept no responsibility for any such changes

A catalogue record for this book is available from the British Library

Library of Congress Cataloguing-in-Publication data has been applied for

ISBN: 978-1-78994-159-3; eBook: 978-1-78994-158-6

2 4 6 8 10 9 7 5 3 1

Designed by Jerry Goldie Graphic Design

Printed and bound in China by RR Donnelley Asia Printing Solutions Limited.

To find out more about our authors and books visit www.bloomsbury.com and sign up for our newsletters

EDITOR'S NOTE
The tools and materials you may need for each project has in places been shortened to a list of 'SELECT MATERIALS'. These are specific to the technique being demonstrated, but you will find more comprehensive lists of the standard items required for things such as cleaning, repair and preparation in Chapter 3 as this could vary depending on the piece you choose to work on.

contents

introduction 6

chapter 1 **sourcing furniture** 14
- Where to Look 14
- Things to Consider 18
- Delivery 21

chapter 2 **tools and materials** 22
- Safety 23
- Cleaning and Sanding 24
- Stripping 26
- Repair 27
- Paints and Finishes 28
- Paintbrushes 30
- Other Application Tools 32
- Art Materials 33
- Other Tools 34

chapter 3 **the basics** 36
- Preparation 37
- Repairs 38
- Sanding 44
- Stripping 46
- Painting 48
- Sealing 52
- Finishing Touches 57
- Hardware 59

chapter 4 **chalk painting** 62
- Project 1 Two Tone 64
- Project 2 Coral Ombré 68
- Project 3 Texture Bombe 74

chapter 5 **decoupage** 78
- Project 4 Retro Memphis 80
- Project 5 Leopard Love 85
- Project 6 Mint Geometric 90

chapter 6 **furniture art** 94
- Project 7 Hand-painted Floral 96
- Project 8 Abstract Landscape 101
- Project 9 Doodle Drawers 106

chapter 7 **alternative techniques** 112
- Project 10 Blue Mirror 114
- Project 11 Neon Cork 120
- Project 12 Stained Glass 126

chapter 8 **refinishing** 132
- Project 13 Bare Naked 134
- Project 14 Harlequin Oak 138
- Project 15 Fade to Black 143

chapter 9 **staging and photography** 148
- Staging 148
- The Shot 155

resources 157

a big thanks to... 160

introduction

Over the years I have transformed so many pieces of second-hand furniture and I have become very used to expecting the unexpected, but I have to say the opportunity to write this book was the biggest surprise of all. This is very much what furniture refinishing is about to me: realising that anything is possible!

Taking a step into this world can be not only practical and technical but also expressive and creative. I take the most pleasure in combining the two and in this book I would love to teach you the basics of furniture refinishing to achieve a long-lasting finish, while inspiring you to go a bit further with your designs to add a personal touch.

I painted my first piece of furniture aged twelve, when I found an old chair in mum and dad's garage and a pot of bright yellow emulsion going spare. I re-covered the seat in fluffy zebra print fabric using a stapler and even sellotape, so it's fair to say my upcycling skills have improved a little since then. But the best part was knowing that for this forgotten chair, it wasn't the end; and it took pride of place in my bedroom where it was loved for years to come.

I started to get involved with refinishing more seriously after buying my first house. I always liked to walk past it as a child; the door was pillar box red and there was the most beautiful arched window which opened like something from a scene in Romeo and Juliet. Over the years the cottage began to look run down but it was still my dream to live there one day. Behind the overgrown garden and the peeling paint, I could see pure potential and really wanted to rescue it; eventually my dream came true, and I did!

While we renovated the house, I learned so many techniques such as stripping wood, sanding and painting… endless painting! I had fallen in love with the

transformative power of paint and restoration despite all the hard work, and could now use these new skills on furniture in the same way, so it was time to pay a visit to the local auction.

I had a family who had always bought second hand and our childhood home was filled to bursting with unique décor. I remember a mahogany dining table we used to use at Christmas which had balloon-back chairs with green velvet seats; then there was the rustic pine Welsh dresser that my mum still has in her kitchen all these years later. So the idea of second-hand furniture wasn't new to me at all and I was excited to give the auction a try for myself.

At that time, the auction house felt a little intimidating and I wondered what the regulars with their big white vans would think of me turning up in brightly patterned clothes and a tiny car hardly big enough to take anything home in, but I received a warm welcome. I had no clue what I was doing but figured 'What's the worst that can happen?' And right at the end of the day the most perfect table came up; it had a rustic pine top, a drawer in the end and Victorian turned legs which I still remember had already been painted mustard yellow. My hand went up and I stood nervously waiting for the hammer to go down; but when it did, then came the adrenaline rush – auctions are very addictive! I took it home, sanded it down and repainted the legs green; my technique needed work, but at this stage it didn't matter as I had to start somewhere!

Years later I still have the table, and as styles and my taste have changed, I've repainted it over and over again. So this is where my love affair with second-hand furniture started. I like how old furniture has the signature of a previous life or era of design, holding stories and memories from the past, whether it be of the period it came from or the people it has belonged to. It can be painted, restored, remodelled and reimagined, but it's the history it already has and the sentiment of the piece that I will always be drawn to. And ever since I first painted the table, it has reminded me of my first house, first auction, being younger, how I paint a lot of stuff green, and the list goes on. I want the things I surround myself with to have meaning and to really say something about me; brand new flat-pack just doesn't have the same story.

We are all unique and our homes are a form of personal expression; how we express ourselves within them is important and refinishing furniture is a great way of doing this. As I mentioned, vintage pieces already have so much character on their own merit that sometimes you don't need to do anything at all; but the more I began to add in my own creativity, the more I realised I was able to make things that were completely individual. The process of putting your own stamp on something feels more rewarding than buying mass-produced and I loved how transforming something old into something new created this really interesting mix of different styles: eras gone by given a modern twist and someone else's vision combined with yours.

I had studied Fine Art at university and so the creative element in my degree came in handy when planning my furniture projects. However, I was a complete novice at refinishing furniture in the beginning and learned as I went along. Piece by piece I soaked up different techniques like a sponge and experimented in my home. I was passionate about the decor and refinishing the furniture properly; for me it wasn't a case of bodge jobs or even being thrifty (although of course it helped me to save money, being a mum of three!). But mostly, I wanted my home and the furniture within it to stand the test of time, as it had already survived up until this point – even though some pieces were a bit worse for wear when I found them! I was less concerned with budget-friendly quick fixes and more focused on creating pieces with longevity – I guess you could say it's a modern version of restoration – and it avoids the temptation to buy mass-produced flat-pack furniture which often falls to bits when you fill the drawers with too many clothes!

On a more serious note, let's talk global warming. It really is happening, so what can we do to help? Now more than ever reducing the amount of materials we consume is important if we want to reverse some of the damage already done. So how can renewing Grandma's chest of drawers (the one we feel a responsibility to keep even

when it doesn't suit the decor) protect the planet? It's not as complicated as you might imagine… by manufacturing less and therefore reducing waste. I think the best way to think about this is that if an old chest of drawers is saved, a new one no longer needs to be produced; and reuse and recycling avoids so many issues that have a negative environmental impact, such as cutting down trees in the first place, modern material production like manufacturing plastic, chipboard and MDF, and then shipping these materials overseas. All of these things increase our carbon footprint, so appreciating and using the materials we already have right in front of us, instead of producing more, can only be beneficial for the environment. More often than not, second-hand pieces are much better quality anyway than buying brand new, so furniture refinishing is definitely a very achievable step towards sustainable living and prevents us staying part of the throwaway society we have become so used to. I have always felt that no matter what our style and taste, it can only be a good thing to keep something in circulation, and in most cases you can reimagine pieces of furniture again and again. I have painted furniture and then stripped it down to bare wood, but whatever the design choice, in every case the result is the same; getting the maximum use out of something for as long as possible.

When I first started doing this as a job, I could never have imagined the roads this profession would take me down, but as my business began to develop I realised it was much more than just furniture refinishing. There are so many rewards: creativity, innovation, respecting what we already have and of course raising awareness around what we waste on a daily basis. It has been such a positive experience for me personally and I am looking forward to sharing with you this world of hidden potential!

Lastly, and before we get to the fun part, the projects… I really would love to challenge the idea that furniture refinishing is a quick fix. I will use cautiously terms like budget makeover and trash to treasure, terms that likely wouldn't be used in conjunction with a skill such as carpentry or restoration; instead I will aim to highlight furniture refinishing as a skill and an art form. I hope to draw attention to the time, effort and care that can go into it; however, that said I am excited about showing you the ropes if you have never tried it before, because it's so rewarding and also a lot of fun.

Think museum worthy and not trash worthy, long lasting not throwaway, and your furniture transformations can be as the title of this book suggests – *Better than New* in so many different ways.

Some past projects...

Yellow Bedside Cabinet
This project uses metallics alongside the chalk painting technique shown in Project 1. The bright yellow and gold balance contemporary with traditional.

Retro Record Cabinet
A mid-century cabinet makes the ideal blank canvas for a masking tape design as in Project 14. I experimented with more organic shapes and colour on this piece by ripping the edges of the tape.

Floral Sideboard
One of my favourite pieces and the original inspiration for Project 5, this felt less like upcyling and more like artistry!

Green Textured Chest
Not quite all it seems, the drawers look like carved wood but are actually textured wallpaper as in Project 6. A chalk based paint effect gives an aged and traditional look.

Neon Drawers
A neon beauty painted in 2019, and framed in black; the first time I felt brave enough to put my abstract artwork out there, as in Project 8, which is a more subtle take on abstract painting.

chapter 1

sourcing furniture

WHERE TO LOOK

If you were not lucky enough to inherit a family member's mid-century sideboard, then you'll have to begin searching for the perfect piece of furniture yourself. But don't worry – as it turns out this is my all-time favourite thing to do. Honestly I think I'm addicted and it has never been more straightforward to find second-hand items nowadays with online marketplaces in abundance!

That said, refinishing, restoring and upcycling furniture is becoming much more popular, so I have definitely had to look a little bit harder for the good stuff lately. For example, sometimes I pay a little more for things and I have also found myself considering previously painted items with more damage to repair as viable projects, as you will see throughout this book. Either way there are always great pieces out there looking for a new home, and if you are prepared to do a little extra work to them the results can be really rewarding.

So where do we begin? Here are my top places to search for furniture treasure…

LOCAL AUCTION

Auctions run regularly in all areas of the country and are a great place to find a substantial selection of furniture under one roof. You can view everything before bidding, so it's a great place to go if you don't know what you are looking for at first; you can really gain experience of pricing and the different styles of furniture available. I'd say an auction is probably the most exciting place to buy, as it depends on who is in the room or bidding online as to how much a piece goes for – if you catch it just right then you can grab a bargain. Auctions are also ideal if you are searching for a piece by a particular designer, because they usually publish their own catalogue online beforehand, which can save you time if you are looking for something specific. An auction is also the perfect place to find a real mix of antique, vintage and contemporary furniture to suit a wide range of budgets.

EBAY

eBay is likely a family favourite in many households – I think most people will have either sold or purchased something on this huge online marketplace at some stage! There are thousands of sellers all under one virtual roof advertising second-hand or pre-owned furniture for sale, and actually it's where I started to source and sell my furniture many years ago. Using this platform is really useful to get an idea of what something is worth and you can search specifically for an item as and when you need it. One of my favourite things about this is the 'add to favourites' feature where you can save your favourite searches; this means you will get an alert when a new item is listed, so you don't miss out on that perfect piece you have been trying to find for ages!

FACEBOOK MARKETPLACE

This platform has gained so much popularity in recent years. Savvy furniture hunters can find vintage pieces at very reasonable prices and with little complication; it's a super-easy way to buy something, as long as you are prepared for a no-frills service. Once you've taken something home then it's a done deal – there are no refunds or exchanges on Facebook and you'll probably have to clean away some cobwebs too! I suggest checking the photos thoroughly before handing over any money but prices are usually low enough for you to take a chance. Items are often listed for collection locally which makes this a great platform to source furniture if you are limited for transport. It's basically a giant virtual garage sale selling a huge variety of household goods and sometimes you can even find things for free.

CAR BOOT

As a kid I remember getting dragged to car boot sales with my parents and now I look back I'm glad of the experience, as I am definitely a better bargain hunter because of it! I mean, what's not to love about sorting through people's unwanted stuff from the back of their cars? It's a great place to find unique vintage homeware that no-one else will have! I'd recommend getting there early and then it's very much pot luck as to what you may find. I have sometimes gone home empty handed but luckily they are fun to attend regardless – but make sure you go prepared with enough cash in case you see the cupboard of your dreams; sunscreen or wellies depending on the weather; plenty of bags to carry home your second-hand finds (a rucksack is handy); and, crucially, enough space in the car to take things home! There are no guarantees, but prices are low and you can negotiate on price if you are brave enough: go on, I dare you!

CHARITY SHOP

You may think of ripped denim jeans or cuddly toys when I mention charity shop, but charity shops are increasingly seeing unwanted furniture dropped at their doors and better still they will even collect pieces people no longer want. There are even special stores dedicated to just furniture and household goods. These are personally one of my favourite places to shop, because not only do I feel that I'm helping the environment by keeping vintage furniture in circulation and it means I'm not buying new; I also love the idea that my purchase is a donation to charity each time. There are always some great items to be had due to house clearances and the stock changes all the time, so be sure to pay them a visit regularly to see what you can find.

AT THE ROADSIDE

Imagine driving or walking along, minding your own business and then from the corner of your eye you see furniture left at the side of the road. Surprisingly, it does happen and I'll often take any opportunity when I can to save things because I'd hate to see them go to landfill. There's something about the sadness of an item left there unloved that just makes me more motivated to perform a rescue mission. However, keep in mind that just because it's free doesn't mean it's always a good idea. Inspect everything carefully and be mindful of the condition before you make the decision to take something away, as often there's a good reason it's in the rubbish pile! In the past, though, I have found some really nice things and have been known to squeeze a table and chairs in the back of the car with the all the kids in tow. So it's worth keeping your eyes open but always remember to get permission from the person throwing it out first.

FRIENDS AND FAMILY

I have often been surprised at the generosity of friends and family, even neighbours and colleagues. If you are struggling to find a furniture project, it's a good idea to ask around to see if anyone has an old piece of furniture sitting in the garage that they no longer need.

In my experience, people are usually really happy for you to take on their project rather than it remain unused or unwanted, so it's always worth asking. Once people realise you like to refinish second-hand furniture, believe me, you will have a queue of people wanting you to take their stuff and more often than not you would be doing them a favour!

THINGS TO CONSIDER

I'm a wishful thinker and believe it's possible to overcome most issues in the world of furniture refinishing; as I keep saying, a problem is only something to solve and the possibilities are endless! However, I have compiled a list of the biggest things that have influenced my decisions when looking for new projects. I hope that you find it helpful.

CONDITION

Since I sell furniture for a living, condition is an important consideration because it has an impact on the amount of time a piece takes to refinish which, if you are selling it on, will affect your profit. It also can affect the desirability of something. In an ideal world a piece of furniture would be previously unpainted and in great condition, but these days pieces like this are harder and harder to find so I am always prepared to do any work required, particularly if it's a really unique piece. I definitely feel that the elbow grease is worth the effort if something is a one-off and, let's face it, most vintage furniture, although mass-produced in its day, will often be unique if it has made it this far! It's important not to discount furniture that needs a bit more effort, as most issues are fixable with the right knowledge and expertise, and to save as much as we possibly can sometimes it's worth doing that bit extra!

Condition, though, is quite subjective. I'd say some people really like the character of a vintage piece and therefore don't want to cover up any wear or tear as with restoration; others like a brand-new look and therefore repair and smooth over any signs of use. I personally use both approaches, depending on the style of the piece, or on whether you want a modern look or a rustic finish, and of course you can mix the two! I'd suggest the biggest thing to keep in mind overall is functionality, as there is nothing more annoying than a wobbly leg. So here are my tips to keep in mind when you are sourcing a piece of furniture.

I am starting with the most annoying – woodworm – as it can really ruin all your hard work if left to go unnoticed. One of the first things I'll do when buying any piece of furniture is flip it upside down to look for holes. Check the feet, base, backboard and bottom of drawers of your piece, as in my experience these are the most common places to uncover holes and where the bugs like to hang out. Left untreated these pesky creatures can eat all the way through your masterpiece. Remember, though, all is not lost; it's reasonable to expect to see this on a Victorian piece of pine for example – unavoidable sometimes if something is that old – but the key is making sure it's treated and stopped in its tracks.

Inspect drawer runners, hardware and hinges, as these are not always straightforward to replace and will affect the functionality of the piece. For example, do the drawers close properly? Usually you can easily fix this by waxing or sanding down the drawer; however,

if they don't fit into the frame well and are tilting back this could be a sign of broken runners and an awkward problem to solve. My advice would be to get quite physical with the furniture, open everything up and see what needs attention. With cupboard doors, discover if these close with no problem; if they don't, it could be a result of moisture in the wood causing warping – again a headache for a furniture refinisher, so keep an eye on that too. Equally, an old hinge that is damaged and hanging off is inconvenient to replace, as is a missing handle – this usually means replacing all of the handles, not just one! Replacing hardware can be really costly and also a design decision that perhaps you do not want to make. Lastly, always look for an original working key, as this is an added bonus; again, they are hard to replicate and having the original will save you time and money. (See Chapter 3 for hardware.)

Does the piece stand level? I recommend pressing down on the top of the item and rocking it from side to side to see if the structure is solid. This will often depend on the style and whether the piece has dainty, delicate legs or a really solid base, but check for any signs of repair or modification underneath. Sometimes you can just screw legs back in securely, which is an easy fix, but legs which have cracked or been sawn down in years past can be challenging to sort out.

And, lastly, this might seem odd, but check for smells, because these are very hard to remove, particularly the smell of tobacco or mothballs; these spell trouble and can be hard to eradicate, so keep this in mind. Furniture refinishing is such a glamorous business!

CHARACTER

With second-hand furniture I always look for a unique selling point, a feature that makes it stand out from the crowd. I guess what attracts you to something is a personal choice, but I look for the authentic personality of a piece and what makes it special compared to something mass-produced. Does it have a retro look or is it more country farmhouse? Why would I buy this over something modern or, just as important, what can I do to a piece to add more character? This might be revealing some natural wood by stripping away varnish or painting raised carving to make it pop. My personal checklist when I'm selecting a piece to refinish begins with have I seen it before, is it unique? Then I try to single out its features, such as hand-carved sections, stunning original hardware, a beautiful shape, or turned legs; I also consider what material the piece is made from and how I am going to make the most of it.

MATERIAL

My dream piece is always going to be made from solid wood: it's sustainable, strong, very forgiving and easy to work with and there are some beautiful old patinas out there waiting to be revealed from underneath sticky brown varnish, as you'll see throughout the book. With wood you can play around with both paint and restoration, fill and paint over or sand right back to reveal the natural wood grain. A mix of the two can also look very effective and I really like that solid wood makes this option possible and doesn't back you into a corner with your design choices. It will also last longer than artificial creations such as MDF and particle board which are problematic to repair and reuse; and there is less risk of damage than with veneer. Wood veneer can be really pretty sanded but it's just a lot more delicate to work with and tends to break. Keep an eye out for veneer that has lifted up on the edges of drawers and doors or for patches of bubbling. All is not lost, though, if this happens, it can be repaired; or you can paint over the damaged areas as part of the design.

When sourcing furniture it's highly likely that you'll come across previously painted items. These will need stripping right back in most cases to achieve a good finish, even if you just want to change the colour it can add hours onto your project; but on the positive side, these can be cheaper to buy, so the extra work can be worth it. Painted furniture is in our past and future, so rather than disregard, I will always give it a chance. Sometimes I even like to use the old finish to my advantage as an extra base layer in rustic pieces, depending on the final look I'm going for.

I will always be happy with a solid wood find. However, for a furniture artist it isn't truly sustainable only to consider one style of project when there are so many styles of second-hand furniture out there waiting to be reused. Items can be made of materials such as plastic, metal, laminate and chipboard, which are more complex to work with but not impossible. There is a huge range of specialist products available to help you deal with tricky surfaces, so I think it's good to stay open-minded and give it a go; I've even upcycled glass before, so everything is pretty much possible! The trick here is to think outside the box, as this will widen your search, and as a result, keep even more pieces of furniture in circulation.

DELIVERY

So you've found the piece of your dreams. What next? Well, fingers crossed you bought locally, so it's just a case of putting it in the car or carrying down the road and I have been known to do this – the neighbours are always

giving me funny looks! Otherwise couriers are an option and can get your treasures where they need to be; this will open up a much bigger world to you when sourcing your projects. It's sometimes pricey but well worth considering, especially if you have seen something you really love but it is miles away. I would definitely recommend using an independent courier who will offer a more direct service; these services can take a little longer to get to you but insurance is included. I would suggest getting a quote from a website like Shiply as a start, and over time build up your courier contact list, saving your favourites and then using them next time.

I hope that this has been helpful and you now feel excited to begin furniture hunting. As mentioned you can even do it from the comfort of your own sofa. Everything is so accessible these days and not only can we source furniture easily to buy for our own projects, we can also rehome items if we no longer have a use or desire for them – so it's a definite win win.

In the next chapter we will look at all the tools you may need to get started on this journey. See you on the other side!

chapter 2

tools and materials

Developing your own collection of tools and materials can sometimes be an investment but this will make all the difference to how amazing your furniture projects look and function at the finish line; Anything that will help the process to run more smoothly, especially the sandpaper (excuse the joke, had to be done) will be a welcome addition when you are in the midst of furniture refinishing; plus the more tools you have, the more possibilities!

Organised into sections, here are listed most of the things you may need to make a good start for each element of furniture refinishing. Aim to build these up as you go along, and I will also include a specific list of tools and materials for each project as we go through the book.

SAFETY

First things first: make sure to check the manufacturer's advice when using any tool or product. As a general rule, I would recommend working in a well-ventilated area, and where possible keep on hand safety goggles, heat-resistant gloves, respiratory masks and a lead-testing kit.

TIP

Prior to the 1960s many paints contained high levels of lead, which has since been found to be harmful. It is a good idea to test samples from older pieces and refer to an official organisation for guidelines on how to deal with it. I base my own precautions on UK advice but this might vary in other countries, so is not laid out in the book.

CLEANING AND SANDING

Even if the can of paint tells you otherwise, I like to think you can never go wrong with prep, as the more effort you put into the preparation, the better your final result will be. The exception to the rule, I guess, is when you are looking at a more characterful finish such as a textured or painterly look; in these cases the prep isn't quite as important. But generally speaking, all second-hand furniture, modern or old, tends to be filthy, so cleaning first is essential for all types of paint. I would recommend you make a start with the following:

DEGREASER/ CLEANER

This is a pre-mixed spray-on cleaner. It will help to remove any grease and grime left on the surface of furniture which could interfere with adhesion.

LINT-FREE CLOTH

Perfect for cleaning, but also for buffing or reapplying wax and wood oil. Using a lint-free cloth will avoid getting particles of fabric or dust in your final finish.

KITCHEN SPONGE

There is no need to buy a specialist sponge, just a humble kitchen sponge will do for cleaning. You may also find these useful for other things such as painting and waxing.

After cleaning, sanding is the next job (though sometimes this might be done after stripping). It will smooth out imperfections, strip back layers, or simply prepare the surface for paint to adhere to. You can choose to go electric for speed and power, or hand sand with a sanding block or flexible sanding pads for precision and a gentler approach.

SANDPAPER

Sandpaper is always graded from coarse through to super fine. For sanding furniture here is a list of the grades you would usually use:

Coarse	40–60
Medium	80–120
Fine	150–180
Very Fine	220–240
Extra Fine	280–320
Super Fine	360–600

The key is to use multiple grades when sanding, starting from a lower grit and moving upwards to achieve the finish you want. As a general rule, if you are looking for a flawless finish, only ever miss out 1 grit in between: for example you could jump from 120 to 180, but not from 120 to 220!

REMOVING

For paint or varnish removal, I would usually start with a coarser grit such as 80–120, moving down to the finer grades to finish.

PREPARING

To prepare wood for painting, the sanding process can be more gentle, so I might begin with 120 grit depending on the state of the surface and go right up to 180 to provide a key for the paint to grip to.

FINISHING

It is not always necessary to use the finer grits; however, if you are looking for a super-smooth surface, especially for applying wood finishes such as stain or oil, it can help to achieve an even more flawless finish. Typically I also like to use a 240 grit sandpaper for sanding in between coats.

ELECTRICAL SANDER

An electrical sander makes light work of sanding, particularly the random orbital sander, which has a vibrating mechanism; it will sand down wood quickly and evenly, and is a good all-rounder, definitely my preferred choice for flat surfaces. So called because of its triangular mouse-like shape, the mouse sander has a back and forward movement which I'd say is less effective than an orbital, but good for small areas and getting into corners and details. Both of these sanders are used with detachable sanding discs. I'd also recommend getting an interface pad, a flexible sponge pad designed to fit onto your sander, which allows you to sand rounded edges, or the curved contour of wooden legs. Lastly, it's worth considering a belt sander for much heavier work, for example where you want to take away a substantial amount of the surface, but I rarely need to use one of these.

DUST EXTRACTOR

A unit which can be attached to your sander via a hose. When sanding it will remove dust particles from the air, creating less debris and also cleaner air quality. These are a good idea if you are working indoors.

SANDING BLOCK

Perfect for hand sanding and a more gentle touch. Covered in sandpaper these distribute sanding pressure evenly and give you a bit more control than sandpaper alone.

SANDING SPONGE

Use for curved and finer detailing such as the spindles on chairs. These are flexible and will wrap around or bend into tricky areas. They can also be washed and reused to save on waste.

TACK CLOTH

Use after sanding to pick up any dust and dirt on the surface of your project before painting or sealing. A tack cloth will trap particles inside the fibres due to the tacky surface, helping to create a super-smooth finish.

STRIPPING

For old pieces of furniture that have been covered in multiple layers of paint or varnish, stripping them first may be a better alternative to sanding alone. Removing the main layers can ease the sanding process, but equally stripping can be a more gentle solution for a project where you are trying to avoid damage to delicate surfaces, such as veneer for example. Whether you decide to strip or sand very much depends on the piece you are working on and what you are trying to remove; at times you may end up using both techniques together to get the best result.

HEAT GUN

This emits heat powerful enough to melt old paint layers or varnish to the point where it softens and can be stripped away. I would advise wearing a heat-proof glove.

PAINT STRIPPER

Paint stripper comes in liquid form. This is convenient when working with intricate mouldings; it is also a gentler approach and a more sympathetic way to reveal natural wood. Although this method can be messy and time consuming, it is sometimes worth it, depending on the project.

WIRE WOOL

A flexible metallic material, ideal for cleaning and polishing small details such as hardware and removing the old finish from wood or metal, and handy to use on detailed sections that sanding cannot reach. As with sandpaper, you can buy it in different grades such as fine, medium and coarse.

WIRE BRUSH

More rigid than wire wool with thicker steel bristles. I like to buy the toothbrush-shaped versions which are helpful for precision paint removal on tricky areas such as beading.

METHYLATED SPIRITS

A solvent which is great for cleaning up wood, or removing varnish. Use after chemical stripping to remove any sticky paint residue or to dissolve varnishes before refinishing. Alternatively you could use white spirits, but make sure to wear gloves.

CARBIDE SCRAPER

A sturdy scraping tool with interchangeable blades, these come in a range of sizes and can strip down large areas in no time at all. They are also useful for getting into corners and details without the mess of liquid stripping.

STRIPPING KNIFE

An alternative to the carbide scraper. Use on delicate wooden surfaces for gentle paint or varnish removal alongside a heat gun or liquid stripper. They are also handy to apply wood filler to projects or strip away paper. Try a plastic version for extra delicate surfaces.

REPAIR

Taking on repairs can open up a whole world of possibilities and give a new life to second-hand furniture that was destined for the rubbish heap. The following products could come to the rescue over and over again.

GLUE

At some point you will likely need to use wood glue. This is suitable for most wood repair jobs, for example fixing a wood joint back together or sticking down broken trim. In situations where the parts that need repair are small, super glue can be a good choice as it is quick drying, and a good option for peeling veneer. Additionally a thick instant-grab glue such as No More Nails can be very handy.

Lastly, you may need more of a gap-filling glue. I would strongly recommend a two-part epoxy because the consistency is a lot thicker, and being resin based it will provide an extra-strength bond with most materials such as wood, metal and plastic. For applying wallpaper or decoupage, use PVA.

APPLICATOR BOTTLE

Applicator bottles are available in varying sizes and are perfect for dispensing liquids. I typically use them to give me more precision when gluing or applying woodworm solution, but you could also use these for paint effects.

CLAMPS

Essential for glue repairs to pull two surfaces together and hold everything in place. I like to have a variety of one-handed bar clamps in different sizes. I would recommend clamps that come with rubber tips to protect the furniture while tightening.

WOODWORM SOLUTION

Woodworm solution is a clear, odourless, non-toxic liquid which is applied onto infected wood. Be sure to follow the manufacturer's instructions and repeat as required.

SYRINGE

To accurately apply glue in awkward spots such as underneath peeling or bubbled-up veneer, a needle-tipped syringe is a handy tool allowing you to get right under the surface. Also good for treating woodworm holes with precision.

WOOD FILLER

I always recommend using a two-part epoxy wood filler when filling holes and cracks that are going to be painted. It is super quick drying, which is a huge benefit. You can sand, paint or drill in 30 minutes.

FILLING KNIFE

A filling knife will help with a multitude of tasks, such as applying wood filler. It looks similar to a stripping knife but the blade is more flexible, allowing you to really push any type of filler into unsightly gaps and holes.

EPOXY PUTTY

This is mixed in two parts and contains an epoxy resin which when set becomes rock hard. I find it useful because of the putty-like consistency, great when you need to fill large voids in wood, or mould missing details to shape such as the corner of something or a broken piece of beading. It is a clay-like adhesive which is waterproof and can be used on pretty much every surface.

SHARP BLADES

Use a utility knife blade or a sharp craft knife for more precision. These will trim away excess paper on decoupaged projects, trim wood veneer or vinyl if required, or remove paint from glass, for example. These can also be the perfect thing to remove dirt that has accumulated in the corners of a piece that a cloth can't get to before painting.

PAINTS AND FINISHES

With so many paint brands out there in a whole range of finishes from matt to gloss, water-based to oil-based, no prep to prep first, it can be hard to limit yourself to just a few brands, and I would really recommend experimenting to find your favourites. However, I want to keep it simple and just recommend the products I use most regularly and the ones I wouldn't be without – hopefully this will give you somewhere to start from!

PRIMER

Primer ensures better adhesion of acrylic-based paint such as eggshell and is necessary when painting troublesome surfaces, typically shiny surfaces such as varnished wood, plastic, glass or metal. It is also stain blocking and helps to eradicate odours.

CHALK-BASED PAINT

This is a versatile water-based and highly pigmented paint which requires very little preparation; however, it will need a topcoat such as polyurethane or wax. In some cases you can get away without priming or sanding so this is often a top choice for a DIY beginner. I love to use it for decorative paint effects such as colour blending and layered finishes or to create texture.

EGGSHELL PAINT

A super-smooth paint with a finish comparable to the surface of an eggshell! I would say the finish is somewhere in between matt and glossy and I love to use it mostly for creating flat finishes. It usually requires a primer and prep, but on the plus side, no wax or extra topcoat. The end result is extra washable and also scuff resistant, making it a perfect choice for busy modern living.

SPRAY PAINT

Use for intricate details like hardware made from plastics or metal. It offers good coverage which is quick drying and free of brushstrokes; and coming in a huge selection of colours it can be an attractive option. Keep in mind that spray paint will not clean up with water and requires good ventilation; but lately I have seen

some water-based options coming onto the market and these are well worth giving a try.

FURNITURE WAX

Use to seal chalk-based paint or wooden surfaces. It comes in different shades and is very easy to apply, providing a buttery smooth finish. The end result is rich and also natural looking; in particular I like using it to intensify colours, and add depth and age to paintwork. Wax does provide a water-resistant surface for a long while after application; however, this tends to need maintaining over time. It's worth keeping this in mind depending on the style of piece you are working on and the function, but I just love the look it creates and would never be without it.

WOOD OIL

Wood oil tends to penetrate deep into the surface of natural wood, and will really enhance the natural beauty and colour; the results still look natural but with a slight sheen. It's easy to apply and you can often achieve a flawless result while creating a protective and water-resistant layer. You will also be able to find or mix the perfect shade for any project. I often opt for a clear wood oil because I like to see the natural colour of wood; however, when finishing wood with orange tones I'd really recommend a white oil which will tone down the natural colour.

POLYURETHANE

Polyurethane is a versatile and varnish-like clear finish to be used on wooden, stained and painted surfaces. Rather than penetrate into the wood, it sits on top, creating a watertight seal. Even if your paint has a built-in topcoat, if your furniture piece is going to be used a lot, for example a table top or a bathroom vanity cabinet, polyurethane can be used to add even more protection to a painted surface. It can also be used for wood on its own. It is a little more complex to apply than other topcoats, but provides the ultimate protection. It generally comes in matt, satin or a gloss finish; and water based or oil based which means you have a lot of options. To apply, I'd recommend using a foam roller or foam brush to prevent brush marks and bubbles.

WOOD STAIN

Wood staining products are useful if you want to either deepen or change completely the colour of natural wood. These come in a variety of colours and can be mixed to create bespoke shades if you are trying to colour match a repair. They are great for hiding small scratches and damaged veneer. Some of these products contain a built-in topcoat, but check the label to make sure; otherwise I'd recommend first staining your wood, then applying polyurethane over the top to fully seal. Alternatively, use a wood repair pen; I like to keep these on hand to disguise minor surface scratches or imperfections, and they're great for adding in fine details.

SPRAY VARNISH

A good option for sealing artwork or smaller details such as painted hardware.

PAINTBRUSHES

It goes without saying but choosing the right brush for the task can really make your life a lot easier. I would thoroughly recommend keeping a variety of different sizes and shapes to use in your projects. But what to choose?

NATURAL

I prefer natural bristle brushes for creating textured, painterly effects so I often use them with thicker products such as chalk-based paints; the bristles tend to be fairly coarse, lending themselves well to old-world looks where you are aiming for more prominent brushmarks. The flexible bristles are very absorbent, helping to distribute paint easily, so they are great for colour blending and getting a large surface painted more quickly.

SYNTHETIC

Synthetic brushes are plastic based so as a result the bristles are firmer and hold their shape better than natural brushes. This makes them the perfect option for precision painting, making it easier to create a uniform flat finish. Use with acrylic based products such as eggshell, primer or polyurethane to achieve an ultra-smooth outcome.

That said, nowadays synthetic brushes can be made to also mimic the properties of natural hair brushes so make sure to experiment with different products to find out what suits you best.

Listed below are some of my essential brushes. There are many weird and wonderful shapes out there; however, these are the types of brush I use most regularly.

NATURAL ROUND BLENDING BRUSH

These rounded brushes are perfect for applying chalk-based paints or wax. Techniques such as colour blending are much easier to achieve due to the soft natural bristles. The shape is designed to hold a lot of paint, meaning you can cover large areas quickly and blend to your heart's content.

SYNTHETIC FLAT BRUSH

You can find flat brushes in a wide variety of sizes to suit the size of the project you are working on. I find them ideal for tasks such as cutting into edges, and detail work when you want to achieve a straight line. The bristles hold their shape and will make it easier to achieve a flat finish while painting or sealing.

LARGE FLAT BRUSH

These are excellent for applying paint washes on furniture, making bolder strokes, and for covering a large area quickly. I would definitely recommend trying these out to see what effects you can come up with.

ANGLED BRUSH

I recommend using angled brushes when doing a flat paint finish as they are ideal for cutting into intricate details, and used on their side will help with getting a straight line; use a smaller version for adding in fine details.

DETAIL BRUSHES

Essential for painting fine details such as trim and carving, or intricate geometric designs. You can also use these for hand-painted details such as floral patterns, as they produce a neat fine line. I like to

BETTER THAN NEW

experiment with different widths and thicknesses to see what marks they create, so I recommend having a good selection to choose from, but the main ones I tend to use are:

ROUND-TIPPED BRUSH

A versatile detail brush which can produce a varying width line as the bristles taper to a point at the bottom. The effect is quite natural and organic.

SMALL FLAT BRUSH

This will create a squared edge and very straight lines, ideal if you are looking for more of a hard-edged and graphic look to your paintwork.

Overall there are many options; with brushes it really is a case of experimenting and finding out what works for you. I do believe, though, that with brushes and rollers, as with tools, investing in better quality usually means they will last so much longer and do a better job. And don't forget to extend the life of a good brush by cleaning them well after every use!

OTHER APPLICATION TOOLS

All the other things you may need to use in your furniture projects aside from paintbrushes!

PALETTE KNIFE

A useful tool to create texture and varying marks on the surface of your work. The blade allows you to spread and layer paint onto the surface, to scrape it away, and to create interesting paint effects.

SPLATTER BRUSH

A very cool brush made from long plastic bristles, which is perfect for creating a splatter effect on paintwork.

BRAYER

A brayer is more commonly used for print making but I enjoy experimenting with this tool to make different effects with paint. Try rolling it in different ways across the surface to see what texture you can create;

you can also use it to smooth colours out. Brayers are particularly effective when using acrylic-based paints and can create some really interesting layers.

FOAM BRUSH OR PAD

Looking for a streak-free finish? A foam brush will help to distribute polyurethane or varnish evenly without any brush marks, will do a great job of covering larger areas and is also handy for applying oils.

WAX BRUSH

It's a good idea to keep a wax brush separate from your other brushes; you can use a natural round brush for this, or you can buy wax brushes specifically. These are good for getting into the tight spots and waxing large areas.

4-INCH MINI ROLLER

These are a convenient size for furniture and can help you to get through a project quickly. They are ideal when painting a flat finish, or applying topcoats to your pieces. I often use a foam roller for topcoats where I am looking for a super-smooth finish, and a short pile roller for paintwork; however, this is down to personal preference. Throughout the book, where I refer to mini rollers, I mean a 4-inch version!

PAINT TRAY

Essential to have on hand to hold paint, and to provide somewhere to lay off your roller. To maintain them as long as possible, make sure you clean out before any paint dries, otherwise you could get little pieces of dried paint in your next furniture project. I'd recommend covering the tray with thick tinfoil before any paint is poured in to make clean-up super easy. I recycle old takeaway trays to hold paint in, too.

WATER MISTER

This creates a super-fine and continuous spray of water, essential for colour blending and paint effects.

KITCHEN SPONGE

Aside from using these to clean with, these are great for applying topcoats for a streak-free finish; or use them to apply a paint wash or to blend colours and create interesting marks. You can also use one to apply wax or wood finishes.

PAINTER'S MASKING TAPE

I would recommend investing in a good-quality painter's tape, which will mask out surfaces you don't want to paint and prevent bleed-through. This can be placed over a painted or papered surface without peeling away the paint beneath it – very useful to create neat finishes or designs and patterns on furniture, or to create neat crisp lines in varying widths.

ART MATERIALS

Having an artistic background, I will often incorporate art materials into my projects. Maybe you wouldn't associate them with DIY or furniture; however, for me it has been so interesting to experiment and add a different dimension to furniture painting. Here are my go-to products to elevate your upcycling from just functional to unique works of art.

ACRYLIC PAINT

Acrylic paint comes in a large selection of colours, is quick drying, and can be applied to a wide range of surfaces from canvas through to wood. The smaller tubes are convenient when adding hand-painted details; or mix them with other water-based paints to intensify the colours.

PAINT PALETTE

I find a paint palette really useful when creating more artistic effects, and will use anything to create one, such as scrap pieces of wood, old trays or containers. Use them for blending bespoke colours or for thinning paint down when needed.

PAINT PENS

Acrylic paint pens can be used on most surfaces and are ideal for applying finer details to artwork with more precision. They are available in a variety of widths.

GESSO PRIMER

In the same way as a regular primer, gesso typically prepares a canvas for painting but you can also use it on wood. It feels a little more substantial than regular primer, with a bit more texture for paint to grab on to, so it's worth having around as an alternative if you want the colours in a hand-painted design to really pop.

WATER-SOLUBLE PASTELS & PENCILS

Perfect either to map out a new design or to add details, lines and extra layers to hand-painted artwork. However, keep in mind these will need to be sealed with a spray varnish afterwards, otherwise they will smudge.

METALLICS

Metallic paints are a lot of fun to use; however, they can sometimes lack opacity, so try to opt for good quality paints. Or you could also experiment with metallic pigments for a more concentrated effect; use gilding wax to highlight details on furniture or hardware, and add sparkle.

SKETCHBOOK

I have a couple of favourite sketchbooks. One is pocket size so I can keep it with me at all times, meaning I can write down ideas or inspiration when I'm out and about. I also like to keep a larger version for painting or drawing practice, but mostly to experiment with colour combinations and write down ideas before committing to a final design.

OTHER TOOLS

Just some of the essentials you may find yourself reaching for!

SCISSORS

Not too much to say about scissors, except make sure you keep them sharp! And useful for a multitude of tasks, especially when decoupaging.

SQUEEGEE

To smooth out any bubbles or creases when applying vinyl or decoupage. Try to get one with a fabric-covered edge to prevent damage; as an alternative, you could use an old credit card.

PAINT CAN OPENER
Never struggle opening a can of paint again with this little tool; it's a game changer.

CORDLESS DRILL & BITS
Keep a drill handy and a varied selection of drill bits for drilling wood and metal. This is an essential tool for re-positioning hardware and also for modifying a piece of furniture, such as adding new legs.

PAINTER'S TOOL
This tool is like the Swiss Army knife of the painting trade, and will help you out on many tasks such as filling, scraping, levering nails and my favourite use, cleaning paint rollers, honestly you must get one and see this magic for yourself!

MITRE CUTTER
If you don't fancy yourself as much of a carpenter, have no fear as this tool is relatively foolproof for cutting thin wooden trims and beading, and works like a pair of scissors, except for wood! So handy, you will be amazed! (As seen in Project 10.)

TACK LIFTER
These are typically used in upholstery, but they are so handy for removing hardware and nails from old furniture.

ADJUSTABLE SCREWDRIVER
I have accumulated a good number of screwdrivers in various forms. However, if you are just starting out I would definitely recommend getting an adjustable screwdriver at first; these have interchangeable heads, meaning you will always have the right attachment for the task.

PLIERS
Pliers come in all shapes and sizes, but these are again useful for removing hardware.

BRADAWL
You could use a very small screwdriver instead, but a bradawl is the official term for a tool that will punch an initial hole in wood, making screws or nails easier to insert.

chapter 3

the basics

It's true that no two pieces of second-hand furniture are ever exactly the same. You will always be presented with a new set of challenges, depending on the life something has led previously. However, you will notice throughout this book that there are some basic considerations and techniques which you will use time and time again on all shapes, sizes and styles of furniture. I repeat these processes a lot through the projects that follow, so I am hoping that by going into a little more detail here, I will provide you with the necessary tools to take on any piece of furniture you wish with no fear whatsoever!

PREPARATION

Good preparation is the key to ensuring a long-lasting and durable finish. It does depend on the look you are trying to achieve and the paint you decide to use, but preparing a piece of furniture properly for any kind of furniture refinishing is rarely a bad idea.

CLEANING

The first step in any project: clean, clean and clean again! Even if you happen to be using a paint brand requiring no sanding prep, it's still good practice to clean your furniture piece inside and out first. The aim is to get rid of any grease and dirt which could affect the adhesion of your final finish.

YOU WILL NEED

- Degreasing cleaner
- Kitchen sponge
- Bowl of warm water
- Lint-free cloth

1. Give your piece a good vacuum down to get rid of any dust sitting on the surface.

2. Use a water-based degreaser and a kitchen sponge to remove any grime. (You may want to wear gloves for this step.) I like to use a kitchen sponge so that the scrubbing part can be used to remove stubborn patches of dirt; however, mostly you will be removing dirt that you can't see – it's surprising what can be sitting on the surface without you realising! Keep a bowl of warm water handy to rinse out your sponge as you go.

3. Continue to clean the outside, inside and reverse of the piece using the degreaser. Once you've cleaned all the surfaces, use a dry lint-free cloth to wipe away any moisture.

BETTER THAN NEW

REPAIRS

You will likely run into a lot of repairs during your refinishing journey, some big and some small, and it would be impossible to cover absolutely everything in depth. However, here are a few techniques that I have used many times. I have singled them out here because time and time again they have rescued a piece with a very strong chance of going to landfill. If you learn how to do these particular fixes it will open up a whole new world of furniture that many people might have dismissed as not worth saving.

WOOD FILLING

This is essential to create a good surface to paint on. Filling will allow you to swap hardware around, smooth over unsightly scratches and even rebuild missing details. I would always recommend a two-part epoxy-based wood filler. This dries quickly, making it easier to complete your projects in record time; plus it is much harder wearing than standard wood fillers and will set rock hard, so it is ideal to fill not only scratches and holes but also larger areas of damage. Using the products and techniques below will help you to cover all bases.

SMALL REPAIRS

YOU WILL NEED

- Two-part epoxy wood filler
- Filling knife
- Sandpaper
- Sanding block *optional*

1. Check your furniture piece for surface scratches, small splits **(a)**, old hardware holes or any missing areas of veneer needing attention.

2. Mix together the two-part epoxy wood filler according to the manufacturer's instructions **(b)** and use a filling knife or the filling tool provided to apply the filler into the damage, pushing it right down into the hole or scratch and making sure it is full of product **(c)**; then scrape away the excess. Work quickly as the filler we are using here dries out at rapid speed.

3. Once the first fill is completely dry, hand sand the filler level with a sanding block and sandpaper, sanding until the area is perfectly flat.

4. If, however, you can still see imperfections on the surface, you may need to repeat the earlier steps. This can happen due to shrinkage as the product dries, particularly when filling a larger hole, but a truly flat surface can be achieved with another layer of filler.

THE BASICS

LARGE REPAIRS

YOU WILL NEED

- Disposable gloves
- Epoxy putty
- Sandpaper
- Sanding block *optional*

1. First check over the piece you are working on for areas of missing beading, broken sections and large holes or splits which will need repair **(a)**.

2. Next put on a pair of disposable gloves and following the manufacturer's instructions, remove the amount of epoxy putty you will need from the pack. It comes in two parts which I mix thoroughly using my hands. Keep pressing it together until both parts combine and you can no longer see streaks in the putty; the consistency will feel a little like modelling clay.

3. Press the mixed putty into the area you want to repair. You can use your fingers to mould it into the right shape, adding a tiny bit of water to help the putty stick and smooth out the surface. It's a good idea to overfill the damaged area ever so slightly because it can then be sanded into shape later. Leave for 24 hours to fully dry.

4. When the putty is rock hard to the touch, sand down flat to the surface, or carefully shape any areas that need it with folded sandpaper **(b)**, and you are then ready to paint **(c)**!

BETTER THAN NEW

REPAIRING PARTICLE BOARD

Particle board is not always deemed the most desirable of materials to work with and, let's face it, working with solid wood is so much easier – but I really don't like to see it thrown on the scrap heap. It was used as a substitute for natural wood after the war and is made from a mix of scrap wood and resin heated up and pressed together to form uniform sheets. The sheets are often covered in laminate to look more expensive; however, as a result it is not easily recycled, so I am always thinking of ways I can reuse responsibly. Particle board typically fails where it has been in contact with moisture **(a)**; where this has happened, the board expands and bubbles up, making it hard to fix. In addition, it doesn't tolerate being nailed or screwed multiple times and tends to disintegrate, but I have found it is possible to repair it using the following method.

YOU WILL NEED

- Stanley knife
- Sawdust
- Wood glue
- Filling knife
- Epoxy putty
- Knife
- Sandpaper
- Sanding block
  Optional

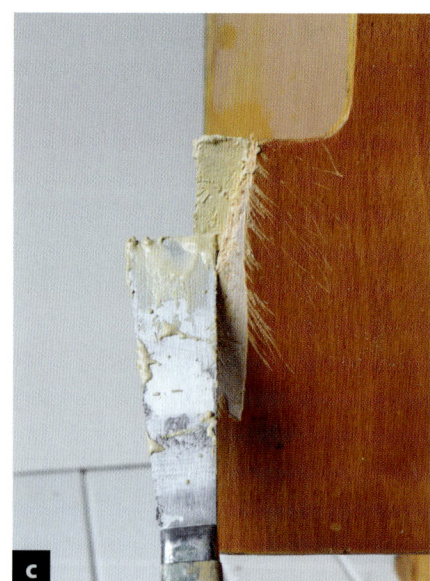

1. First sand down the bubbled area flat. If the damage is more drastic, cut away the loose flaky parts of failed particle board using a Stanley knife, until you meet material that doesn't crumble away **(b)**. This process looks quite drastic, as if you were breaking up a well-known breakfast cereal, but don't worry about that at this stage!

2. Then seal in the exposed particle board by mixing sawdust and wood glue to make a strong paste; press into the cracks using a filling knife **(c)**, or your fingers; then leave to dry overnight. The idea is to stop the particle board from flaking away.

3. Once the glue mixture is completely dry, use epoxy putty to fill in the missing area **(d)**, following the steps in Large Repairs above, and sand down as normal.

WOODWORM

Probably one of the most off-putting things about old furniture is woodworm. It's right to be cautious, but treated correctly the problem can be solved, and speaking as someone who really loves a rescue mission, it seems so wrong to throw away decent furniture when all it needs is some time and some woodworm solution. Plus, for some, woodworm holes are an accepted sign of history and character, particularly with antique pieces that already have rustic appeal. As long as the problem is treated carefully, there is no real reason why furniture with this issue should be overlooked, so here's how to fix it.

YOU WILL NEED

- Disposable gloves
- Respiratory mask
- Woodworm solution
- Container
- Old paintbrush
- Needle-tipped syringe

1. First turn your piece of furniture into a convenient position. When you apply the liquid, it will need to soak down into the holes, rather than just running out of them, so consider turning your project upside down or sideways so you can really make sure the woodworm solution can soak in and do its job.

2. Ideally put on gloves and a mask. Pour some of the water-based woodworm solution into a container where you can get better access to it. Take an old paintbrush and flood the surface where the holes have appeared, paying particular attention to cracks, crevices, joints and anywhere where something could be hiding from you **(a)**. Repeat until the surface is fully saturated and be really liberal with this step to ensure that there is plenty of solution in the gaps, then wait to fully dry out before going any further.

3. If you feel it is necessary, you can also use a needle-tipped syringe to apply the woodworm solution into each hole **(b)**. This takes patience but will ensure that everything is treated properly. Then leave the wood to dry out again. (I personally like to do another full treatment after this stage just to make sure.)

4. When the project has completely dried out you can fill the holes and refinish. Alternatively, leave them as they are to add character; it really depends on the style of your project and the look you are going for.

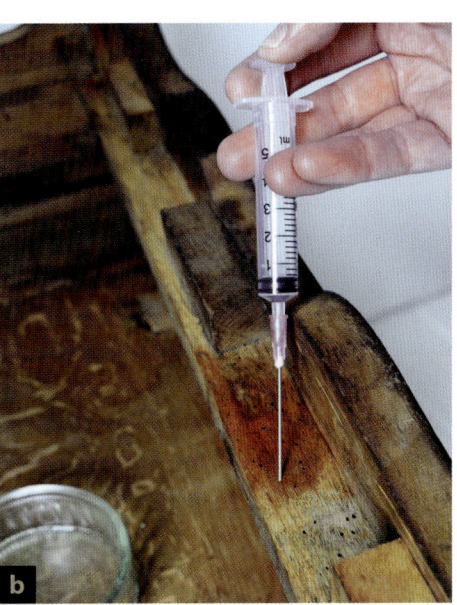

TIP

To detect woodworm, check the underside, the legs and the bottom of drawers, the places where a piece of furniture meets the floor. If you see holes, tap this area over some white paper: and if sawdust falls, then you know the woodworm is still alive and needs treating.

REPAIRING VENEER

Have you ever been put off buying or keeping a piece of furniture because of peeling or chipped veneer? I have often found furniture on the scrap heap because people don't know how to fix it. Veneer is a paper-thin sheet of natural wood normally applied onto cheaper timbers, and as it's so thin, it has a tendency to either lift up or snap. Some may see it as a cheaper alternative to solid wood; however, I see a lot of quality furniture covered in beautiful veneers – it's a stunning material to work with and brings with it so many possibilities in the world of furniture design. So let's fix it!

BROKEN VENEER

If you notice a piece of veneer lifting up **(a)**, rather than ripping it away, which can be very tempting, instead preserve it and try to glue it back down. You will get a much better finish by doing this and once it's sanded flat again nobody will ever know there was even a problem!

YOU WILL NEED

- Wood glue
- Small brush
- Applicator bottle
- Masking tape
- Fine sandpaper
- Sanding block *optional*

1. Carefully pull away the damaged piece of veneer without snapping it to reveal where you need to glue **(a)**.

2. Cover the area with wood glue using a small paintbrush and/or use a small applicator bottle **(b)** to get the glue into the cracks.

3. When everything is covered, press the veneer tightly back into place and secure using masking tape pulled tightly across the damage **(c)**.

4. Wait for this to dry, then peel away the masking tape. Sand the repair down with fine sandpaper and you are good to go.

THE BASICS

MISSING VENEER

1. Glue down the damaged veneer edge with super glue **(a)**, securing it with masking tape; this will stabilise the damage and stop any more moisture from getting underneath. You could use a small piece of wood or a flat tool to press down the veneer as the super glue dries, to get the veneer flat while avoiding getting any glue on your fingers.

2. Once dry, use a two-part epoxy wood filler to fill in the gap **(b)**. Choose a shade of filler closest to the colour of the original wood grain and apply.

3. Once it is completely hard, give the filler a light sand down using fine sandpaper, blending the damaged area into the rest of the veneer. Hand sand carefully so as not to damage any more wood, making sure the repair looks completely flat.

4. Next, I like to use paint to fill in the damage and match it up to the colour of the existing veneer. I use acrylic paint and mix different colours together to achieve the desired shade, then paint onto the repair using a fine paintbrush **(c)**.

5. You can also try mixing up wood stains to hide the repair, and wood stain pens are handy to draw in any grain lines using a similar colour to the existing finish **(d)**. Then, once everything is dry, seal the area using your chosen topcoat and no one will ever know!

YOU WILL NEED

- Super glue
- Masking tape
- Two-part epoxy wood filler
- Fine sandpaper
- Acrylic paint/wood stain or pens
- Detail brush
- Chosen topcoat (please see pages 52–6)

TIP

If you have a large area of veneer to replace, try real wood veneer which can be cut to shape and applied to furniture. You can then blend in the correct wood colour using the steps above.

SANDING

As a general rule, I would say sand everything to get the best finish you possibly can at the end. Whether you are painting your project or refinishing natural wood, it is essential most of the time. The sanding process does the following:

- Smooths out surface scratches and imperfections
- Roughens up an old finish so that paint will adhere more easily
- Strips away dirt, paint and varnish to reveal the surface underneath

SANDING SAFETY

Be sure to wear a respiratory mask while sanding and work in a well-ventilated area at all times. If you can't take your project outside remember to open the windows. I would also recommend investing in a dust extractor to remove any particles as you work! Where in doubt, consult a reliable website for further safety information around sanding.

ORBITAL SANDING

For flat surfaces such as drawer fronts, the top or sides of a project, I would 100 per cent recommend a random orbital sander. This will get the job done quickly and will leave you with a smooth and even finish. To get the best results, follow the steps below.

1. After cleaning and filling, next select the correct sanding disc for your orbital sander. There is more information about sanding grits on page 24, but generally:

    - For preparation sanding (when painting): use a finer-grit sandpaper to lightly scuff the surface evenly. The aim here is to just scuff the old finish to give paint something to grip onto, without going right through to bare wood, which can create uneven patches in your paintwork.

    - For deep sanding (when refinishing wood): begin with a coarser grit and then move up through the grades to a finer grit to achieve a smooth surface and a topcoat without imperfections.

    - Make sure to line up the holes with the base plate, as this is where the dust will be extracted from. If using a dust extractor, make sure it is attached securely. Be sure to wear safety glasses and a mask to protect yourself from any dust particles.

2. Place your orbital sander on the surface, start it up and then move very slowly in the direction of the grain, all the time applying an even pressure and holding it flat to the surface of your project **(a)**. Try to avoid tilting the sanding plate or pressing too hard on it to avoid damage to veneers or unsightly circular sanding marks which occur when the sander is working too hard. The sander should glide across the surface rather than be forced.

3. Hand sand any details that the electrical sander can't get to using sandpaper **(b)**. Try using a sanding block for flatter surfaces or a sanding sponge for curvy details depending on the project.

YOU WILL NEED

- Safety glasses
- Respiratory mask
- Orbital sander & sanding discs
- Sandpaper
- Sanding block *optional*
- Sanding sponge *optional*
- Dust extractor *optional*
- Tack cloth

THE BASICS

SANDING BY HAND

It is tempting to go straight for the power tools because you will see results quickly, but I would still recommend hand sanding for the following tasks:

- Scuff sanding – lightly scratching up the surface to provide a key for paint to adhere to
- Delicate details – a gentle approach for smoothing and sanding around contours or carving and dealing with finer material such as veneer
- Finishing – hand sanding leaves behind fewer scratches than a power tool, so is useful for the final sand to create a flawless finish (once the bulk of the sanding has been completed)
- Fine sanding – in between coats of topcoat or paint to achieve a super-smooth surface

4. Once all the sanding is done, use a tack cloth to lightly pass over all the sanded surfaces **(c)**. This will pick up any dust particles left behind, which means you are now ready to apply your chosen paint or topcoat.

BETTER THAN NEW

STRIPPING

So why strip furniture? Believe it or not, it can sometimes be a more gentle process than sanding and is perfect for exposing intricate details, revealing delicate wood grains and removing multiple layers of paint. That said, it is likely that light sanding will still be beneficial after the stripping process. However, if this is the case the process will be less harsh on the surface beneath, and a lot easier.

USING A HEAT GUN

My favourite tool for removing multiple layers of old paint. Although this method can be time consuming it feels quite therapeutic, as the process is instant and the clean-up is a lot easier than with liquid stripper.

1. When using a heat gun, it's definitely a case of safety first. Use heat resistant gloves to protect your hands and find a well-ventilated space to work. Be sure to wear a respiratory mask to protect yourself from any fumes.

2. Turn on the heat gun and hold about an inch or so away from the surface, being careful not to scorch the wood. You can direct the heat exactly where you want it until the paint begins to bubble **(a)**; check to see if varnish has softened using your scraper, as this can be harder to see.

3. Hold the scraper at an angle to the bubbling paint or softened varnish and glide along the surface in one direction with the grain, taking the finish off in long strips if you can **(b)**. Be careful not to gouge the surface of the wood during this process – if you feel this might happen, switch to a plastic scraper. The paint will likely come away in curls, and once dry these are easy to clean up using a vacuum; I find this easier than dealing with the sticky mess produced by liquid stripping.

4. For intricate details, I like to use a small wire brush with a gentle action to remove the paint or varnish stuck in cracks and crevices. Wire wool or folded sandpaper also works well for this step.

5. Keep in mind that you don't have to remove every scrap of paint unless you are stripping it back to bare wood. As long as the main bulk is removed, the sanding process afterwards will create a surface flat enough for you to paint on. Continue to clean and sand the surface ready for painting or for applying a new topcoat **(c)**.

YOU WILL NEED

- Heat gun
- Heat resistant gloves
- Respiratory mask
- Carbide scraper or stripping knife
- Plastic scraper
- Small wire brush, wire wool or sandpaper

LIQUID STRIPPING

Messy, but my preferred method when I am refinishing something with an odd shape or a beautiful wood grain because the liquid stripper will get right into all the details; also ideal when working with delicate materials such as wood veneer, as it will minimise the level of sanding that is required afterwards. Nowadays you can find solvent-free, super-strength liquid strippers which will work on any surface but without the horrid chemicals. Just check the label and experiment until you find the right one for you.

YOU WILL NEED

- Plastic sheeting
- Protective gloves
- Respiratory mask
- Paint stripper
- Disposable trays
- Old paintbrush
- Stripping knife
- Small wire brush
- Medium wire wool
- Methylated spirits
- Degreasing cleaner
- Kitchen sponge

1. Set up your project in a well-ventilated space and protect the surface you'll be working on with plastic sheeting as this can be a messy job. Then put on some protective gloves and a mask and pour your chosen paint stripper into a disposable tray.

2. Apply the paint stripper liberally to your piece using an old paintbrush **(a)**. You should be able to see the stripper sitting on top of the surface; once done, leave it to work its magic according to the manufacturer's instructions. I usually wait an hour or so before checking back.

3. You will know if the process has worked when the paint or varnish has bubbled up or softened. At this point remove the residue with a scraper or stripping knife **(b)**; or use a small wire brush to get into any details **(c)**, and use another disposable tray to offload the residue as you go through the process. Reapply coats of stripper as required, repeating the steps above if needed.

4. Once most of the finish is removed, I recommend removing any other residue left behind with some medium wire wool and a dab of methylated spirits **(d)**, making sure to rub along the grain of the wood. Do wear gloves for this part.

5. Finally, wash down your piece with degreaser and a kitchen sponge then let it dry completely overnight. Once it is dry, you can continue to lightly hand sand the surface as in the earlier steps if you still feel it needs it.

PAINTING

Where would we be without paint? There would certainly be less creativity around, but it's not always about pretty colours and a painted design; getting the hang of good painting techniques can be the difference between a successful project and a complete disaster. So here are some basics to make your furniture projects go without a hitch.

MASKING

When my piece is fully cleaned and prepped for paint, the last step before getting started is to mask out any areas I want to avoid getting paint on. Masking can be helpful when you want to create a neat and professional finish and will avoid my own personal worst nightmare of opening up a drawer only to find paint drips on the edges! The key to this step is to avoid using poor-quality masking tape and invest in a professional-quality painter's tape. You can also use painter's tape for more artistic tasks such as colour blocking and creating geometric designs.

> **YOU WILL NEED**
> - Painter's masking tape
> - Small flat brush
> - Clear polyurethane or paint

1. Make sure the surface you are working on is clean and dry so the tape will stick properly.

2. Line up your tape against the edge you want to mask out **(a)** and press down firmly, using your fingers to smooth out any air bubbles.

3. To avoid bleed-through, apply a tiny bit of clear polyurethane or paint (in the corresponding colour) using a small flat brush, depending on the finish you are taping up; this will create a seal between the tape and the surface underneath it to prevent any product from seeping underneath. And once dry, you can begin to paint.

4. When the paint is dry to the touch, remove the tape slowly and at an angle to get a crisp line **(b)**.

PRIMING

Priming is an essential step when using certain paints as it helps the paint adhere properly to the surface. However there are many different paint brands on the market, so it is worth checking the manufacturer's instructions to see whether priming is actually going to be necessary. I'd recommend using it on anything that is shiny or glossy, such as laminate, metal or heavily varnished items, as it helps with adhesion. Primer is also stain blocking, so will help to cover wood tannins and ink stains, for example. My favourite is a multi-surface, water-based primer as this will stick to most surfaces and is compatible with most paints, and the clean-up is also easy; however, consider using an oil-based version for more heavy-duty prep. You may notice me using grey primer when painting with darker shades and white for paler colours; and you can also use a clear primer when you don't want a colour to show through from underneath, for example when you are distressing a piece of furniture.

As a general rule I would use primer for:

- High traffic areas
- Painting with pale colours
- Tricky surfaces such as laminate or plastic

In my opinion skipping priming is okay if:

- You are working on rustic timber
- You aim to achieve a distressed or textured finish
- You are using a suitable no-prime paint

YOU WILL NEED

- Tack cloth
- Primer
- Painting materials

1. First make sure the surface you are priming has been prepared and cleaned if necessary.
2. Following the manufacturer's recommendations, apply coats of primer as required **(a)**.
3. Once the primer is dry, you will have the perfect base for painting.

TIP

If using brighter or darker colours, try tinting your primer with your chosen paint colour first to help with coverage.

USING A ROLLER

I would recommend using a roller for painting large flat areas. These are a good option for achieving a professional flat finish, and will avoid any imperfections or visible brushstrokes in the paintwork when used well; they also get the job done more quickly! You can choose from a selection of different thicknesses but generally I find a short pile roller ideal for painting old furniture as, while smooth, it will still do a good job of covering up old and rustic wood grains because it has a tiny bit of texture. When working on smooth surfaces such as laminate, you might instead consider using a foam roller with a smoother surface.

YOU WILL NEED

- Paint
- Paint tray
- Mini short pile roller or foam roller
- Fine sandpaper
- Tack cloth

1. Pour an amount of paint into the reservoir of the paint tray, making sure it doesn't overflow onto the textured half. To save time on washing up you can first line your tray with tinfoil but this is optional.

2. Roll the roller backwards and forwards into and out of the reservoir, spreading the paint onto the textured area of the tray, until you have a fully saturated, but nice and even coating of paint **(a)**.

3. Paint one side of your project at a time; starting just away from the edge, begin to apply paint to the surface, going with the grain from the bottom to the top, then back again **(b)**. Avoid forcing all of the paint out of the roller as this will create lines in the paint. Your roller should be loaded up enough to glide across the surface without you having to press too hard. Gradually work your way across the piece in a uniform fashion from the top to the bottom until the whole section is covered.

4. Once covered evenly, use the unloaded roller again to lay off the paint. This is the process of softening and hiding any visible brushstrokes. I start with the roller at the furthest edge and with zero pressure just go back over the surface to smooth down any imperfections. It's important to travel in one direction from end to end to eradicate any lines or ridges of paint, creating a smooth, uniform finish.

5. When the paint has dried fully, I sand very lightly between coats before applying another coat of paint in the same way. Do this by passing over the surface gently with fine sandpaper, removing any more dust created with a tack cloth.

6. Repeat the steps, leaving adequate drying time in between coats until you get full coverage.

TIP

Before using a roller, wash it out with water, then wring it out well so it is damp and not dripping. This will help the paint to soak into the pile, for an even application.

THE BASICS

USING A BRUSH

I mean, rollers are great, but there are plenty of times when using one isn't the best option when it comes to painting furniture, and I would favour a brush any day of the week. I like to have both options on hand as brushes are versatile and can achieve many different effects. They are perfect for the furniture refinisher and the DIY'er but also for the artist. I would recommend using a brush for the following tasks:

- Smaller projects
- Creating a textured or blended finish
- To hand paint bespoke designs
- Cutting into edges
- Painting rounded or curved details
- Getting into tight spots
- Painting intricate details such as beading or carving

For a smooth finish, the principles are pretty much the same with a brush as with a roller. Remember to repeat the processes such as laying off and sanding between coats to get your paintwork really smooth.

For a hand-painted finish, you can take a much more random approach and really anything goes, so don't sweat the small stuff. You can find more information on the variety of brushes available in Chapter 2.

AVOIDING DRIPS

It is always my mission not to have any paint drips or runs when painting furniture; so here's some tips on how to avoid them:

- Make sure your paint is thoroughly mixed together by giving it a good stir, which prevents the consistency being too watery.
- Don't overload your paintbrush, just cover the tip of the bristles rather than the entire brush and remember to offload any excess on the edge of the can before beginning to paint (a good cheat to prevent the edge of the can becoming clogged up is to secure a piece of masking tape or stretch a rubber band over the top of your can, and wipe the brush on this).
- Always try to work in a well-lit space where you can see what you are doing. The times I have 'missed a bit' when I just couldn't see properly…
- Don't run before you can walk – take it slow and build up light layers rather than trying to achieve full coverage in one go. Wait for each light layer to dry fully before beginning the next. Even if the surface looks patchy, it will come good the more layers you add, I promise!
- Inspect your work over and over again, rotating it to check corners and details, regularly smoothing out the drips as you go. Even when you think you have finished, look over your work one more time to check for any drips that have occurred.
- If you happen to find a drip once your project has dried, don't fret, just use some fine grit sandpaper to sand it out again, and then repaint.
- Lastly, I like to avoid drips by using a roller as much as I can, especially on large flat surfaces as brushes have more potential of overloading the surface with paint.

SEALING

It can be hard work prepping, stripping and painting furniture, so standing the test of time is essential. A topcoat helps to seal wood, paper or paint, providing a durable and practical finish and making your piece of furniture fit for everyday life. There are a few options you can choose, depending on what you are using your project for, and the style, but the methods below I find myself turning to again and again.

WAXING

Furniture wax is a great all-rounder and I love to use it for both its decorative and practical benefits. It's a versatile protective topcoat that can really take the look of a painted finish to the next level, but will also seal and bring out the beauty of natural wood. While wax does provide a good degree of protection, I would recommend topping it up every so often to keep your projects fully protected. So why choose wax over other topcoats? I guess for me it's much more than just a topcoat and can hugely transform the look of a piece of furniture as well as sealing it.

WAXING OVER PAINT

I like to use wax over a chalk-based finish as part of my creative process. It comes in a variety of different colours and can be useful in creating light, shade, age and character over your paintwork. Here's how:

YOU WILL NEED

- Clear wax
- Black wax
- Wax brushes
- Kitchen sponges
- Lint-free cloth

1. Apply clear wax to the surface in a circular motion using a wax brush **(a)**; this will ensure the product gets everywhere and into any imperfections on the painted surface. I like to work on one side at a time. The clear wax will act as a base so that you can adjust the colour and depth of the darker wax we are going to use in the later steps. Without this first layer applied, the darker colour will stain your paintwork and it will be harder to blend the waxes.

2. At this stage the colour of the paint will have deepened but the surface may still look quite matt, even patchy. Don't worry about this; once the wax has settled for a few minutes, wipe off any excess with a lint-free cloth. Try not to let the clear wax dry too much, as we want it to still be wet and workable for the next step.

3. Then apply black wax with a separate brush or a kitchen sponge. I concentrate on any areas of interest, for example the edges, the legs, the carved areas and around hardware; however, there are no rules. This step can look quite scary but have no fear – give it just a minute or so to penetrate into the surface, then rub away the excess lightly with a lint-free cloth. As a result the paintwork will lighten up again and the darker colour should have settled into creases and crevices,

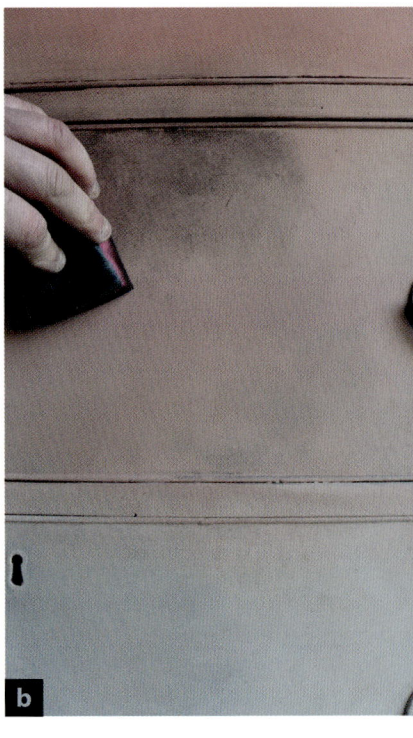

giving an authentic time-worn look. If you find that you still have too much dark wax on your project, go in with a little more clear wax which will act like an eraser.

4. To take this effect a little further I recommend reapplying black wax over the already shaded areas, using a kitchen sponge for more precision. Go over these with your sponge, using more of a dabbing motion and blending the darker wax into the lighter areas to add more depth **(b)**.

WAXING NATURAL WOOD

You can also use wax as a finish for natural wood. It will bring out the patina and give the surface a soft-looking natural sheen. This works well for farmhouse-style pieces where you may want more of a matt finish.

YOU WILL NEED

- Wax
- Wax brush or kitchen sponge
- Lint-free cloth

1. First make sure any previous finishes are completely removed to enable the wax to penetrate the surface **(a)**. If replenishing something that has been waxed previously, this is not necessary unless you want to completely change the colour.

2. Once the piece is clean, apply your chosen colour of wax to the whole surface in a circular motion with a wax brush or sponge **(b)**, getting into all the nooks and crannies. I would typically use clear wax to enhance natural wood, but consider darker waxes for more of a rustic look; and in this project I am using white wax to lighten the orange tones in the pine.

3. Remove the excess wax with a lint-free cloth and buff the surface to a shine **(c)**.

POLYURETHANE

There are many different types of polyurethane, whether it be gloss, satin, matt, or a wax effect finish, so you will always find the perfect version to suit you. This is a versatile clear topcoat which is non-yellowing, and will protect your furniture really well from daily use. It is different from wax, oil and stain because it sits on top of the surface rather than penetrating it. As a result, it creates a tough watertight layer and I love to use this on top of a painted finish, sealing in wood stain or applied to decoupaged panels.

YOU WILL NEED

- Water-based polyurethane
- Paint tray
- Foam brush or foam mini roller
- Fine sandpaper
- Tack cloth
- Flat brush *optional*

1. First read the small print. Each product varies, so be mindful of what the manufacturer recommends in terms of ideal conditions and re-coat times.

2. I use a water-based clear polyurethane which comes in a variety of finishes. Pour some product into a clean paint tray and use a foam brush or foam roller to apply **(a, b)**; using foam for this step will prevent brushstrokes – however, you can still use a flat brush if you prefer.

3. Make sure the surfaces you want to seal are completely free from dust using a tack cloth and that your foam roller or brush is clean; then brush on your topcoat from side to side, and section by section. Don't be tempted to apply product in every direction, as this will overwork and cause an uneven appearance at the end.

4. Work relatively quickly, making sure not to push down too hard on the brush or roller to prevent bubbles forming on the surface. The varnish should just glide on, and once you have a section covered, do a final long stroke lightly from end to end to lay off the topcoat and eradicate any brush marks.

5. Make sure any drips are smoothed out and leave the surface to dry completely. Then continue to apply multiple coats of polyurethane as required (sanding very lightly between each layer with fine sandpaper and removing the dust with a tack cloth).

TIP

If sealing a painted surface, add a touch of the same paint colour into the polyurethane to tint it. This may seem strange but will help to avoid the white marks you can sometimes get with clear topcoats.

STAINING WOOD

I use wood stain when refinishing wood to alter and enhance its colour. It comes in a huge range of shades which can be mixed together if needed; this can be useful when matching in repairs where two colours don't match or for covering scratches. Occasionally, stain can come out blotchy, particularly on softer woods like pine, so I would recommend using a wood conditioner to achieve a much more uniform effect. This isn't always necessary but worth keeping in mind.

YOU WILL NEED

- Pre-stain conditioner *optional*
- Applicator such as foam brush, kitchen sponge or lint-free cloth
- Wood stain
- Small brush
- Top coat (polyurethane or oil)

1. After the wood surface is fully prepped and free from dust, you can opt to apply pre-stain conditioner to help the wood stain soak in evenly. (I would recommend doing this on raw soft woods to prevent blotchy patches; however, on harder or pre-stained woods, this isn't necessary.) If relevant, apply pre-stain conditioner, with an applicator of your choice; I prefer to use a lint-free cloth, a kitchen sponge or a foam brush. Use long strokes in the direction of the grain to apply evenly, avoiding any pooling of product and leave to soak in.

2. Then use a clean applicator of your choice to stain the wood with wood stain **(a)**. Apply your desired colour liberally but using the same process as in Step 1.

3. Wipe away the excess stain with a fresh lint-free cloth to reveal the finished effect. A deeper colour can be achieved by applying more coats of wood stain as required.

4. You can also use wood stain to match up an existing colour on your piece of furniture, by mixing together different stains. I tend to do this on the piece by layering up different colours until I get the perfect shade, but feel free to test on a scrap piece of wood first.

5. Let the wood fully dry before applying your chosen top coat such as polyurethane or oil **(b)**. This will add proper protection and also enhance the depth of colour.

TIP

When covering small scratches or imperfections, apply wood stain with a small paintbrush for more accuracy.

OIL

Oils penetrate wood deep down, replenishing and enhancing its natural colour and patina. I use oils to draw attention to the wood grain on areas such as legs, handles and table tops and it's the perfect finish to bring out the natural beauty. Even if light scuffs occur on the surface through time, these can easily be undone with a further application of product. But bear in mind that there are many different versions of wood oil, so check the manufacturer's instructions before applying to see which one suits you.

YOU WILL NEED

- Tack cloth
- Disposable gloves
- Foam brush or kitchen sponge
- Wood oil
- Lint-free cloth
- Fine sandpaper

1. First clean down your piece with a tack cloth and put on gloves to protect your hands. Then put a small amount of oil onto a foam brush or sponge.

2. Apply the wood oil to the surface, working along the grain until the wood is evenly covered **(a)**. The surface shouldn't be dripping with oil; just apply enough to soak into the grain. I like to leave it to soak in for a few minutes.

3. Then wipe off the excess with a clean lint-free cloth, making sure to leave no oil sitting on the surface.

4. Leave the oil to cure for a while according to the manufacturer's instructions, then sand lightly with a very fine sandpaper to smooth the finish down again.

5. Wipe the surface down with a tack cloth to remove any fine dust, and then repeat Steps 2–4 again until you are happy with the level of sheen.

TIP

If the lid to your wood oil gets stuck, pour a kettle of warm water over the seal to loosen.

FINISHING TOUCHES

When I first started furniture refinishing years ago, these are the parts of the process I didn't really want to focus on, because they just were not as exciting as the transformation on the outside! But as time went on I realised that doing some of these small and sometimes overlooked details made all the difference to both the functionality and the quality of each project – it's always the little things that matter.

DRAWERS & RUNNERS

For me there is nothing worse than drawers that stick, and I have found that this issue is often the reason vintage furniture can be discarded. However, it's actually quite straightforward to fix this problem by doing the following:

YOU WILL NEED

- Orbital sander & sanding discs (medium & fine grit)
- Tack cloth
- Clear wax
- Wood oil
- Kitchen sponge
- Lint-free cloth

1. First remove any drawers from the frame, remembering what order they went in (I would suggest numbering them in pencil on the base, as old drawers can vary in size).

2. Sand down the interior of the piece and both sides of each drawer using an orbital sander and sanding discs. The aim is to take away some of the surface at first, so begin by using a medium grit sandpaper and move down to a finer grit to finish. Sanding will neaten up the sides and also prevent the drawers from sticking later.

3. Vacuum the whole piece to make sure there is nothing left behind from the sanding process, and wipe all the interior areas down with a tack cloth to get rid of the sanding dust.

4. To replenish the interior, apply either clear wax or wood oil with a kitchen sponge **(a)** and wipe away any excess product with a lint-free cloth. I find this will freshen everything up yet keep the character of the piece.

5. Next, I like to apply clear wax to the outside edges of the drawers, using the same method as before **(b)**.

6. Lastly, apply wax onto the freshly sanded runners and the sides of the interior **(c)**. Slide the drawers back in, and they should now glide really easily.

THE BACK

For the back of the piece, I like to rub down the wood with fine grit sandpaper, just to smooth it down and get rid of splinters on the edge; then use a tack cloth to remove the dust. Lastly, apply oil or wax as before to replenish the wood and keep things neat and tidy.

KEYS

Some of the pieces you will be working with are likely to be quite old, and it's common for vintage furniture to come without a key, but you can search for second-hand keys online; it is often possible to find them in job lots on second-hand marketplaces like eBay, so keep your eyes peeled! I always keep a collection of these stashed in the workshop and when I need an old key, I just give them all a try and take my chances!

LINING DRAWERS

On the right project, a decoupaged interior can be a nice touch, and can also cover a multitude of sins (if you are dealing with damage or ink stains, for example). This handy hack for lining the inside of drawers is a good option to have just in case; and of course you can use this technique on the backs of cabinets or doors to add a personal touch.

TIP

Keep an eye out for maker's marks and labels on the reverse of a piece or on the inside of drawers. These show the history of a piece of furniture and add character so try to preserve them if possible.

YOU WILL NEED

- A4 card
- Masking tape
- Wallpaper
- Sharp scissors
- Flat brush
- PVA glue
- Clear polyurethane
- Foam brush

1. First lay four pieces of A4 card into your drawers, pushing each piece into the edges. If you are working on a larger drawer and the card doesn't overlap, just add more pieces of card until the base is fully covered.

2. Stick down the pieces quite securely with masking tape before removing the cardboard from the drawer **(a)**. This should now form an exact template of the drawer base.

3. Place the wallpaper you are using pattern side down onto a flat surface, and place the template on top. Draw around it carefully with a pencil and use sharp scissors to cut out.

4. Using a flat brush, paint PVA glue onto the base of the drawer **(b)**, then take your cut-out piece of wallpaper and press it down carefully onto the glue. Smooth the paper outwards from the middle, pressing out any air bubbles.

5. Leave this to dry overnight and then seal to protect with polyurethane and a foam brush as in the earlier steps **(c)**.

HARDWARE

One of the things I love about working with vintage furniture is the amazing hardware. The old designs are often unique and usually great quality too. I like to keep original details when I can as it maintains the character and authenticity of the final project. However, sometimes there are situations where replacements can be a better option – for example, in cases where you have a particular look in mind and the old hardware doesn't suit, or where handles are broken or missing.

So, will you keep the originals or opt for new? Here are some things to consider.

ORIGINAL

The reason I am attracted to buying a piece of furniture in the first place is often purely the hardware! It can be the heart and soul of a vintage piece and add character and provenance, so think carefully before removing old handles. A finish can be changed at a later date, but once features such as handles are discarded, these can't be replaced. Appreciating what is already there or reinventing it will also save time and resources!

REPLACEMENTS

But of course there are occasions where replacing hardware is a much better option! New handles can change the look of something instantly and there are many designs available, from carved wood to ceramic and metal in every shape, colour and size. You can even find replicas of old designs. So why choose new?

Firstly, a whole new set is perfect for modernising a piece; it's also not uncommon to come across furniture with a few handles missing, so replacing the lot is usually the best way forward as it can be really hard to find the exact same design! But keep in mind that replacements can sometimes be costly and you may also have problems getting the new handles to look authentic, depending on the look you are going for; a nice touch is to source vintage handles online that are more in keeping with the age of a piece. You can find quite a large variety of pre-used hardware on second-hand auction sites. Sometimes I've even found an exact replica, particularly with the more mass-produced designs, and this can actually add value to a sought-after piece.

REVIVING HANDLES

If at first glance handles look tired and worn, even rusty, don't be put off as there are many different ways you can revive them. Decide whether you want to fully clean them or to keep some of the aged patina, or even paint them to change the colour – there are so many options.

CLEANING

It is truly amazing the way in which metal hardware can be transformed with careful cleaning. I would recommend using either a metal polish or the following vinegar technique to clean tarnished hardware and bring it back to life. Personally I find a combination of the two works quite well.

a

1. Having removed the hardware from your project, place it in a container and cover with boiling water, then add a teaspoon of bicarbonate of soda and a really decent splash of vinegar **(a)**. Give it a stir (keeping in mind that the solution will bubble up at first) then leave to soak for 30 minutes to an hour.

2. Remove the hardware and rub the metal clean using a kitchen sponge (you could use fine wire wool for more stubborn patches), then wash away any residue under the tap.

3. Dry everything off, polish up using a clean cloth (see below), and in no time at all you will have super-clean hardware **(b)**.

b

YOU WILL NEED

- Container
- Boiling water
- Bicarbonate of soda
- Vinegar
- Kitchen sponge or fine wire wool
- Metal polish
- Lint-free cloth

PRESERVING

Make the most of the original patina. This is a thin layer that naturally forms on the surface of metal and wood through age and exposure and once this is removed it's very hard to replicate. I avoid cleaning the hardware fully if I'm working with a traditional-looking project; instead I try to preserve the natural age, using just a layer of wax and a sponge to apply, then buffing the hardware back to a shine.

POLISHING

YOU WILL NEED

- Metal polish
- Kitchen sponge or fine wire wool
- Lint-free cloth

1. Dab a pea-sized amount of metal polish onto a kitchen sponge or some fine wire wool. Rub across the metal hardware in small circular motions until the grime starts to loosen **(a)**.

2. Buff to a shine with a clean cloth, and just like magic the metal underneath should start to appear **(b)**!

PAINTING

You could also consider painting hardware. It's a great way of adding a contemporary twist to a piece of furniture, and giving a completely fresh appeal to handles that perhaps you are not keen on. As with furniture, handles can also really benefit from a complete overhaul! You may notice a few different ideas throughout the projects in this book, but you will find more specific information about painting handles within Project 11.

chapter 4

chalk painting

I have always been in love with the transformative power of paint. It is truly magical and a paintbrush can hold so many possibilities. But where to start? There is a huge variety of different products on the market, all creating different finishes and requiring different levels of preparation. It can be daunting at times but I'm going to start where I began, with chalk-based paint. With so many different brands out there to choose from, some chalk based, others clay based, and some a mixture, it can get confusing. But whichever brand you choose, all have very similar benefits and starting with this medium is one of the most approachable ways to begin the painting journey, and remains very close to my heart.

The minerals in chalk-based paint allow it to adhere to almost any surface or material, so one of the largest benefits is that your project will need minimal, possibly no prep, depending on the piece. This is what every beginner furniture refinisher wants to hear and means you can get a project started straight away. Prep work is never a bad idea, though, so if you have the time to do it, then great; but if you just want to begin and find the idea of stripping and sanding really daunting, this is a great technique to get you started, with instant gratification.

Personally I don't always prefer a flat finish and this type of paint lends itself well to experimentation. In this chapter I will teach you the basics of chalk painting but I also want to show you how to get a lot more out of this medium; it is such a versatile product and your projects can be about so much more than just a quick colour change. I really love to experiment with creative techniques, such as adding texture and blending to create more complex painterly effects, and I want to show you that this technique can range from simple to much more advanced – your project can be whatever you want it to be.

CHALK PAINTING

project 1
two tone

before

This blanket box turned up while I was treasure hunting in the local second-hand warehouse. To be honest, my workshop was full of furniture and my intention was only to 'look' not to buy. I always say that… but I can never resist an item with such beautiful carving. This gorgeous piece had 'me' written all over it, so it went straight into the boot of my car, as I knew I would never see another. All the curves may not be for everyone but I love the drama and the unique appeal of something like this; the detail was definitely crying out to be painted.

Once I got it home, I found that the the box had been made to look older than it actually was. In my original plan, I was going to attempt to sand the lid, hoping to find solid wood underneath. But after discovering it was mostly chipboard, I decided to paint the whole thing; sometimes with vintage furniture not everything goes according to plan, so improvisation is key!

All in all this kind of item makes a perfect first project, with interesting details to accentuate and very little repair work – it is absolutely ideal for chalk-based paint.

SELECT MATERIALS

- Chalk-based paint (I chose 2 different colours for this project)
- Round blending brushes
- Water mister
- Clear wax
- Black wax
- Wax brush
- Kitchen sponge
- Lint-free cloth

1. Start by giving your piece a good clean. (See Chapter 3 for cleaning.) On this rare occasion my project was in a good state of repair. I rubbed it down first with degreaser and a kitchen sponge, making sure to remove any grease spots, dust or grime that could affect the adhesion of the paint to the surface.

2. Consider removing hardware at this stage such as hinges or handles if you would prefer not to paint over them. For this project I removed the hinges with a screwdriver and reused them later.

3. Fill in any obvious large gaps or damaged areas with two-part epoxy wood filler and a filling knife to create a smooth base to paint on. (See page 38.)

TIP

Keep your eyes open for furniture with carved details. These look great when creating a rustic paint finish – chalk paint is perfect for accentuating them.

Use colours with confidence. I suggest experimenting with many different shades to see what works well together; you don't have to stop at just two! Remember, if it doesn't look good you can always paint over it, and the variety can create some really interesting layers.

4. Chalk-based paint doesn't always require sanding, so this step is optional. However, with this project I did remove the old varnish on some of the carved areas; I hand sanded using medium grit sandpaper because I wanted a tiny bit of the wood grain to show through the paint at the end. I use sandpaper here instead of an electric sander to get into the details and awkward spots **(a)**.

5. Use a tack cloth to pick up any loose dust after sanding. The more rustic you want the final finish to be, the less thorough you have to be with this step, but bear in mind that any loose dust can discolour lighter paint colours or create unwanted texture on the surface.

6. Apply a base colour onto your project using chalk-based paint and a round blending brush **(b)**. I tend to paint the areas I want to accentuate, like the edges of the box and some of the carving, keeping my brushstrokes quite random and not covering everything completely. Bold colours tend to work better as a base; I chose a gorgeous dark green which will provide a good deep background.

7. Once fully dry, add a contrasting colour over the top **(c)**. Here I chose a lighter shade to the base coat to create depth. I lightly brushed turquoise over the previously painted areas, with minimal paint on my brush so as not to cover the base colour completely; and still leaving some wood showing through in parts, which gives a lovely rustic look to the chest.

8. You can also use a water mister alongside Step 7, lightly spraying the surface of the paint in some areas to reactivate it **(d)**. This will allow you to play around with thinner layers of paint to add depth and will also create a smoother result. After these steps, you can leave the painting here, or add additional layers if you feel your project still needs it; however, I would recommend letting the paint dry between each coat, so that you don't end up losing the definition between each layer.

9. To seal, apply clear wax across the whole surface of your piece using a wax brush, which will help to work the wax into all the grooves and details **(e)**. (See Chapter 3 for waxing.)

CHALK PAINTING

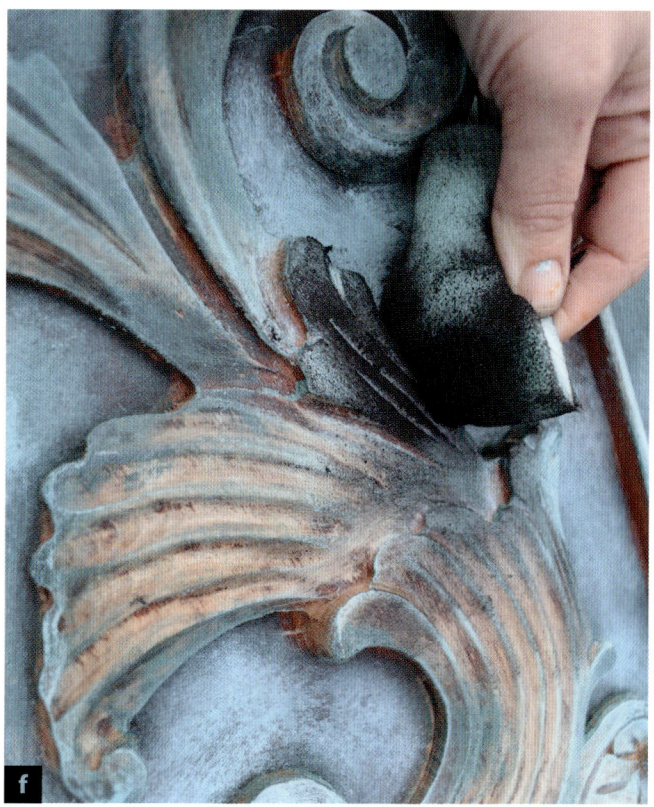

10. Then apply black wax sparingly using a kitchen sponge to get into some of the carving and detailed areas **(f)**. Use your sponge in a circular motion to blend out the dark wax into the lighter spots to create shading.

11. Wipe away the excess with a lint-free cloth. If you feel any areas are too dark, remove the black wax with a sponge and clear wax; this will act like an eraser and rub out the black wax you don't want to keep, it's magic!

12. If you need to do any paint touch-ups on the paint finish, feel free to do this once the wax has cured overnight. It's a common misconception that you cannot reapply chalk-based paint once something is already waxed, but I find that it helps to add texture and depth to the paintwork. Apply the paint again as you did in the earlier steps if preferred, and then wax to seal as before **(g)**.

13. Clean any metal hardware to remove any patches of rust and dirt with wire wool, then use clear wax to restore the patina, buffing with a lint-free cloth to add lustre. (See Chapter 3 for cleaning hardware.) Finally, reattach **(h)**.

CHALK PAINTING

project 2
coral ombré

before

With a chest of drawers this stunning, it's easy to see past repairs. Beautiful, curved drawers and shaped bracket feet make this antique piece really stand out; with something so old, knocks and bumps just add charm and authentic character, which is lucky as it has more than a few of those. Despite the damage, I can see so much old-world charm that a brand new piece just can't compete with. It feels elegant and sophisticated with a Georgian look, so I am thinking about a soft and romantic paint effect and for this, the ombré effect is perfect! The term ombré is a French word meaning shaded; it refers to the subtle shift from dark to light. Imagine a dreamy faded effect, almost like a watercolour sky in appearance, covering the spectrum between two colours. You can really experiment a lot with this, going much brighter and with more contrasting colours, but I wanted to create an ethereal look, showing what can be achieved with just a few shades.

SELECT MATERIALS

- Round blending brushes
- Chalk-based paint (minimum two colours)
- Water mister
- Wax brush
- Kitchen sponge
- Clear wax
- Black wax
- Flat paintbrush
- Lint-free cloth

a

b

1. First, an old item like this usually needs a really good clean after years of use, so I cleaned the whole piece inside and out with degreaser and a kitchen sponge. I also found some old paper liners stuck inside the drawers, which I saturated with water and then scraped away **(a)**.

2. Next, I glued down any loose pieces; here I focused on the beading around the drawers, as this was very brittle and unattached in places **(b)**. Try to salvage what you can and use wood glue placed in a small applicator bottle to get it into any tricky areas. Then I used painter's masking tape to secure beading and trims in place.

3. The missing parts needed something more heavy duty than regular wood filler so I used an epoxy putty to fill in the gaps. (See Chapter 3 for how to use epoxy putty.) With this project, I hand sanded the repairs with a sandpaper to form the shapes of the missing beading.

4. Next, I sanded down some of the wood very roughly. This part of the process is optional as we are using chalk-based paint, but I find an ombré effect works really nicely using this method on a solid wooden surface, and means the wood grain will show up well underneath the paintwork where desired.

5. (Optional) At this stage I also sanded the top fully with an orbital sander **(c)**, and I will refinish this to a natural wood finish in the later steps. (See Chapter 3 for sanding.) However, if you don't wish to do this, paint the top as in Step 6.

6. Grab some round blending brushes for the next stage and keep a separate brush for each paint colour, which will allow you to blend the paint more effortlessly **(d)**. Feel free to experiment with colours here; however, I chose a classic coral pink and white combination to show effectively how an ombré effect traditionally fades in tone

7. Begin with the darkest colour of your selection at the top of the piece, painting a strip on the top third, extending around to the sides. Use a water mister to help spread the paint across the surface if needed. As this is a natural wood piece, I would suggest quite a thin covering of paint and that you apply quite loosely, not worrying if a few bits of wood are missed during the process, as this will add authenticity and natural age to the paintwork.

8. Taking another blending brush, apply the palest colour to the base of the chest in the same way.

9. Then for the middle section, mix a colour between the darkest and the lightest shade (I used coral and off-white in a 50/50 mix). I stir it up in an old takeaway container with a lid so that I can keep this colour fresh in case I need to use it again at a later date; always make sure you mix enough to avoid running out of paint as it's often difficult to mix up the exact same shade.

10. With a separate brush, apply the 50/50 paint mixture onto the middle section of the piece in the same way as before **(e)**. You should now have three stripes of paint and at this point it may look quite messy, but don't worry – we will blend together in the next step.

11. To create an ombré effect, we will need to blur the line where each colour meets the next. To do this, first add a small amount of the darkest colour to the relevant brush, and extend the darkest shade from the top drawer down onto the second drawer. Use a water mister to help you blend each colour into the next but use it very sparingly **(f)**. Move the brush gently from side to side at first, changing to a more vertical motion to spread the paint more evenly if needed. The key here is to gently brush the surface with a very delicate touch until the two colours combine.

CHALK PAINTING

12. Now blend from the other direction, painting back up into the darker colour using the mid-tone colour from the middle section, until you achieve a blend you are happy with. Repeat the earlier steps for each colour transition until each section is blended nicely.

13. During this process, as your brush starts to dry out, drag it subtly over any details or the edges of the drawers and handles to add a little bit of texture to the paint finish. This process is called dry brushing and looks great with an ombré effect, picking out the details of the piece.

14. Next, seal the paintwork; wax naturally creates an ethereal look and adds so much depth. On this piece, think of wax the way you might do a pencil drawing, with all the details shaded from darker to lighter! For this use a wax brush to apply clear wax first and then black wax to follow **(g)**. (See Chapter 3 for waxing.)

15. I decided to paint over the handles with this project as they look much softer against this ombré piece; so all I need to do is reveal a tiny bit of the original brass using a damp cloth and wax over them. I'd also recommend cleaning up the escutcheons on each drawer **(h)** as this makes all the difference to the finished look.

TIP

If the surface of the paint gets too wet while you're painting an ombré effect, sometimes paint can pull away revealing the wood underneath. So use water sparingly. The best thing to do if this happens is to let the surface dry completely and come back to it later.

CHALK PAINTING

WHITEWASHING

If you are painting your whole project, then this is the end! However, as the rustic charm of this project was so lovely, I decided to refinish the top and restore it back to natural wood using a whitewashed effect. This technique is very useful on projects like this to tone down the orange or red tones in old wood such as mahogany, pine or oak.

WHITEWASHING MATERIALS

- Chalk-based paint
- Water
- Container
- Kitchen sponge or flat brush
- Lint-free cloth
- Clear polyurethane
- Foam mini roller
- Paint tray

i

j

TIP

It's not always necessary to repair absolutely everything on an old piece of furniture because sometimes the knocks and bumps are what add character, showing the history of an item. I recommend repairing only the things that you feel detract from the look or the function of an item.

16. To create a whitewashed effect, use a 50/50 mix of paint to water; it should be the consistency of single cream, perhaps a touch thinner. The solution is thin because we are looking to create a translucent wash to knock back the natural colour of the wood ever so slightly, yet still show the wood grain underneath.

17. Spread the thin mixture onto the sanded top using a large flat paintbrush or a sponge **(i)**; work quite quickly here so the paint does not dry out, then rub away the paint again using a lint-free cloth **(j)**, all the time going with the grain in smooth strokes.

18. Once the paint wash is fully dry, seal with clear polyurethane using a foam roller for a smooth and durable finish **(k)**. (See Chapter 3 for sealing.)

k

73

TIP

Metallic pigments come in powder form and I like to roll them into the surface of the wet paint. This makes the colour more intense and creates a really eye-catching effect.

CHALK PAINTING

project 3
texture bombe

before

Honestly, I probably overpaid for this little bombe chest considering the condition it was in, but the classic curvy shape is hard to come by, so I have no regrets! Called a 'bombe' chest from the French word meaning 'curved', this reproduction piece doesn't have a lot of age to it, but does feature that iconic bulge outwards on the front and sides, and I just fell in love with the shape. But this had already been painted a few times, with some quite thick layers which were looking tired, so choosing a rustic paint effect seemed like a good plan. This is a great technique to avoid extensive prep with a pre-painted piece like this one because texture will cover up pretty much everything and I also feel it will suit the French style. As well as incorporating texture, I experimented with metallics and pops of colour in jewel tones; it's very much about experimentation, so when you're in the painting stage and placing down colours feel free to mix up the order of the steps and the tools used, and keep repeating until you get a look that you are happy with. Even the mistakes you make will just form another layer which you can use to your advantage. It's the kind of project where you have that little moment of doubt half-way through, but in the end it always turns out better than you ever thought it was going to. Keep the faith and trust the process!

SELECT MATERIALS

- Chalk-based paint (various colours)
- Round blending brushes
- Bicarbonate of soda
- Brayer
- Flat brush
- Metallic paint
- Gilding wax
- Splatter brush
- Carbide scraper
- Palette knife
- Sandpaper
- Lint-free cloth
- Wax brush
- Kitchen sponge
- Clear wax
- Black wax

1. As I am demonstrating a textured effect here, the prep can be very minimal. Use a sanding block and medium grit sandpaper to give the surface a good key, removing any big paint drips and raised areas. That said, the base layers of paint-jobs-gone-by can sometimes work to your advantage, so keep this in mind if you would prefer to see some of the old texture underneath.

2. For this project I paid extra attention to the drawer runners and edges as they had been previously painted; I sanded them back down flat where paint had started to build up, as this could affect the functionality of the drawers **(a)**. Doing this properly made sure they opened smoothly at the end.

3. To start, begin with a base coat of paint; using a dark colour will add depth and mood to your final finish. Apply the paint liberally and in a random fashion, using a round blending brush **(b)**. This will allow you to stipple the surface and create some chunky texture in places. Stippling could be described as applying paint repeatedly in the same area with small up and down touches, to create a raised effect. Throughout this step, lay the paint on nice and thickly and in different directions to create lots of raised texture. Now leave the base coat to dry fully; this could take a while due to the thickness of the paint.

4. Next, mix bicarbonate of soda with a paint colour that contrasts with the base coat. There are no set rules and feel free to experiment with consistency, but I like to create a mixture about the thickness of cake icing **(c)**. Add as much or as little bicarbonate of soda as you want to create your desired thickness, making sure both parts are thoroughly combined. If your mix gets too thick, thin it down using more paint.

5. Using a flat surface such as an old scrap of wood or a paint palette, roll a brayer onto the surface to pick up the paint mixture, then roll in a random fashion to the front of your cabinet **(d)**. Experiment with applying more and less pressure to get more of an irregular effect, but still leaving some of the original base coat showing through.

6. Again, wait for this to dry, then, using a flat brush and contrasting colours, brush across the surface of the chest; the aim at this stage is to get distinct areas of colour, which is why drying time between layers is important **(e)**. It will look quite abstract but everything should be layered up like a paint sandwich rather than mixed up together like a cake (this is the best way I can find to describe it!).

7. To add even more interest, I suggest experimenting with metallics because these add an extra dimension to the paintwork and will glint and glimmer on the surface **(f)**. I recommend metallic paint – or try brushing gilding wax onto the paintwork; this will catch on all the raised areas and sit in the grooves of the texture nicely. Apply wherever you see fit, paying particular attention to the areas around the hardware, as I always think handles look lovely with a bit of gold on them.

CHALK PAINTING

8. Using a clean round blending brush, paint a single layer of your chosen colour over the previous layers, leaving some of the original colours and texture still peeping through **(g)**. Using a paler shade will create a striking contrast with the colours underneath and make them pop. It is not as important to add any textured strokes here, so paint as normal (as in Project 1).

9. You can also try experimenting with a splatter technique by creating a drippy paint mixture. Use a 50/50 mix of metallic paint to water; dip a splatter brush into the solution and pull back on the bristles to create a subtle splatter effect **(h)**. I like to start doing this once the heavier layers are down, but add more splatters throughout the final steps, if you feel your project needs it.

10. Next, and this bit is magic… use a carbide scraper to gently scrape away some of the top layers, revealing the texture you have been so busy creating **(i)**. Any areas where the paint is raised will come away to expose some of the colours you have created underneath, creating a chippy effect. Scrape away paint where you feel it needs it; I paid particular attention to the edges of the drawers and legs, places where paint would naturally wear. It's a messy part of the process but it's so much fun seeing all the colour popping through.

11. Use a palette knife to add more textured details; with a tapping motion to build up interesting layers in colours that complement each other. I used a bright neon pink **(j)** and finally a lighter shade of green **(k)** to finish everything off.

12. Take a damp cloth and wet distress the handles a little, rubbing away the paint to reveal some of the metal underneath **(l)**. You can then add a touch more gilding wax to accentuate them even further.

13. If you wish, take a piece of fine sandpaper and lightly pass it over the whole piece to knock back a little bit of texture, creating a slightly smoother and practical finish for a modern home.

14. Finally, seal in the paintwork using wax. I use a wax brush to apply an all-over coat of clear wax, followed by black wax to add the illusion of age to the paintwork. (See Chapter 3 for waxing.)

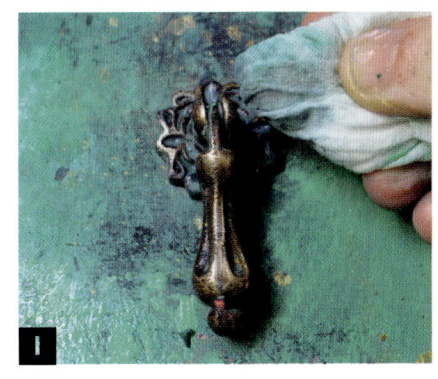

chapter 5

decoupage

Decoupage is a great thing to have in your repertoire when it comes to furniture refinishing. The word originates from the French word 'découper' meaning to cut out. Put simply, it is the art of applying either paper or fabric onto an object with glue, and then adding a layer of varnish to seal. Decoupage is a really good way to update a piece of furniture with eye catching artwork if you are not confident about creating your own designs. Of course you can keep it as simple as applying the paper of your choice, however there are some more complex things you can do with it, to really make the design your own and I will be giving you a few ideas in this chapter. I'll start by simply showing you how to apply the technique, and then experiment with different ways to make it more bespoke. Today there is a huge variety of different materials to decoupage with, such as wallpaper, fabric, made-to-size murals, rice paper, even vinyl; and as we move further into the digital age, an even larger number of patterns, textures and prints to choose from. Eye-catching designs such as bold florals and geometric prints are everywhere these days so I guess the hardest bit of this technique is going to be deciding which design to use! In the past decoupage has had its roots more typically in craft, but it is now becoming popular to use it in more innovative ways to create high-end contemporary designs for our homes.

DECOUPAGE

project 4
retro memphis

before

During a late-night scan of Facebook Marketplace I spotted this huge sideboard. I'm fairly sure it will divide opinion, especially pre-transformation, but I always like to go for unusual things and this piece is a total one-off – one of the huge advantages of buying vintage. It has a retro 1960s feel and I really, really love the chunky square handles. However, the surface is super glossy and quite a few of the parts are made from particle board, which over the years has been exposed to moisture; this meant I had a big challenge on my hands before I could even begin to think about colour and pattern. On the bright side though, the large flat surfaces were perfect for decoupage and the fold-down doors would make a brilliant drinks cabinet. In the end I managed to find this amazing Memphis-style wallpaper, almost like an oversized terrazzo print, and the bold shapes I thought matched perfectly with the retro handles. I couldn't wait to transform this one, as sometimes the most unlikely of candidates can bring the biggest reward.

SELECT MATERIALS

- Painter's masking tape
- Water-based primer
- Mini short pile roller & tray
- Eggshell paint
- Detail brush
- Wallpaper
- PVA glue
- Flat paintbrush
- Utility knife blade
- Squeegee tool *optional*
- Sharp scissors
- Foam brush or mini roller
- Clear polyurethane
- Wood oil
- Lint-free cloths

1. Clean down the entire piece with degreaser and a kitchen sponge **(a)**. With this project I was very lucky in discovering that the interior had a beautiful natural wood patina and that the cabinet doors were Formica backed. I liked the idea of keeping these elements because it gave the sideboard provenance and character, and everything looked so much better after a good clean.

2. Remove the handles with a screwdriver to create a flat surface to work on. I will clean the handles up later as you can't beat original features like this.

3. As the sideboard had sections made from particle board, I was keen to repair these before starting on any other prep. The legs in particular really needed some attention due to previous water damage (see page 40). I'll warn you at this point, things have to get worse before they get better – but don't worry, it will look perfect by the end.

4. Fill the larger areas of damage using a two-part epoxy putty which is mouldable and waterproof **(b)**. Press it into any large voids and mould into shape, cut away the excess and use a bit of water to smooth it out and help the putty to stick. Again, leave this to dry until it's rock hard to the touch. (See pages 39–40) I will sand this smooth later on.

5. While this was drying, I removed the old finish, using a heat gun (wear heat resistant gloves) and a carbide scraper to carefully strip each panel. (See Chapter 3 for stripping.) I removed the paint from the doors and side panels, going with the grain where possible, before moving on to the varnished areas and then the handles. The wood underneath came up beautifully, so much better than I expected!

6. After stripping away the old finish, scuff sand the sideboard ready for paint and paper. Use a sanding block for more intricate details such as the curved sections of the legs and the edges of doors. I decided to keep some natural wood areas on this piece, so used the orbital sander more thoroughly with fine sanding discs to get a super-smooth finish. If possible, adjust your sander to a low speed to avoid wearing through any veneer; then finish off these areas by hand sanding. (See Chapter 3 for sanding.)

7. Use a tack cloth to remove any dust before priming, and apply painter's masking tape to block out any parts you do not want to get paint on **(c)**.

8. After all the prep, we are ready to prime! Using a water-based primer with a mini roller, prime the surfaces to be painted and decoupaged. (See Chapter 3 for priming.) I primed here as in the next step I was going to be using eggshell paint; the need for priming does depend on the paint brand you are using, so check the label first to see whether it's necessary.

9. Once the primer is dry, apply your chosen paint colour. I used an off-white shade of eggshell to complement the paper, as the neutral frame would make the bright colours in the wallpaper really pop. Apply two to three coats of paint using a mini roller **(d)** according to the manufacturer's instructions, leaving appropriate drying time and fine sanding between coats to achieve a silky smooth finish. (See extra instructions on pages 50–1.)

> **TIP**
>
> Decoupage is so versatile. I really enjoy using both vintage and modern wallpaper – the number of new designs available is incredible. However, you could also use paper napkins, rice paper and wrapping paper. Even wallpaper samples put together in a patchwork effect can achieve a show-stopping result.

DECOUPAGE

10. Hold the wallpaper up against the sideboard to get a feel for where it will look best **(e)**. I decided to decoupage the top panels, leaving the bottom third painted to give a colour blocked effect, but placement of the paper will always depend on the characteristics of the piece you are refinishing; and ultimately it's up to you! As vintage furniture is rarely straight, I prefer to avoid measuring and do things by eye, but measuring a central line to work against can be helpful.

11. Apply a medium layer of PVA glue to the surface using a flat paintbrush **(f)**; too little and your paper won't stick properly and too much can cause bubbles under the surface. You want to see a layer of white on the surface but not dripping glue. Be careful to remove any particles of dust or dirt that get into your glue, as these can sometimes be seen underneath the paper. If this happens, try to fish them out using the edge of a sharp blade.

12. Lay the wallpaper down onto your piece of furniture very gently, being careful not to press down straight away, as you still want to be able to adjust it. I start by lining up the straight edge of the paper with the straight edge of the door at the middle point, so each panel will sit evenly in the centre. I use a squeegee tool **(g)**, but you can use an old credit card if you want to or just your hands. Gently press the paper outwards until it sits perfectly flat, smoothing any bubbles. Pay particular attention to the edges, making sure they are stuck down well.

13. Before leaving to dry, press down really hard onto the edges of the piece where the paper will end to create an impression almost like a fold line, and wipe off any excess glue from the paper using a slightly damp cloth.

14. Trim away most of the excess wallpaper with sharp scissors, leaving a slight overhang **(h)**. We will neaten the edge up once everything is completely dry.

15. Continue applying pieces of wallpaper to cover the whole surface, following the earlier steps and making sure each piece slides up to the next with no overlap, continuing the pattern seamlessly.

16. Leaving the paper to dry completely will ensure a clean cut. You can now use a sharp blade to cut away the excess overhang **(i)**. Importantly, hold the blade at a slight angle as shown; this will make sure the paper is cut ever so slightly away from the frame, preventing the paper catching and causing a problem later on.

17. Check that the surface is clean and free from dust, then use a large foam brush **(j)** or a smooth mini roller to apply a clear polyurethane topcoat to the piece. Apply in linear strokes from side to side, and with a light touch to finish each coat. I would suggest four to five coats for a decoupaged project, which will make the papered surface really hard wearing and suitable for use. (See Chapter 3 for sealing.)

18. Seal all the exposed wood panels with wood oil. I used a hard-wearing worktop oil on this project, applying it liberally with a sponge and leaving it to penetrate the surface; after a few minutes, I wiped away the excess with a lint-free cloth and continued to build up more layers according to the manufacturer's instructions. (See Chapter 3 for oiling wood.)

19. Lastly, reattach the refinished hardware to complete the look.

TIP
Before applying wallpaper, prime the surface with a light layer of the paint you are using. Once dry, this will make the wood less porous when the glue is applied and will mean the wallpaper adheres well.

project 5
leopard love

before

A 1930s dark wood cabinet lacking a bit of lustre is a common occurrence when you work as a furniture artist, but can often mean the perfect blank canvas! I was looking for a piece with flat surfaces to demonstrate decoupage effectively and wanted to show how pattern can make such a huge statement to something quite plain. This technique can be likened to painting by numbers, I guess, as rather than just stopping at a pre-printed design, we'll be modifying and making the design our own by painting on top of it to make it look more authentic. Sometimes decoupage can lack a truly unique feel, but adding your own creative touch makes your piece of furniture even more bespoke, and for me this personalised technique creates something which looks very high end; plus leopard print never gets old!

SELECT MATERIALS

- Chalk-based paint
- Short pile mini roller & tray
- Wallpaper
- PVA glue
- Flat brush
- Squeegee or credit card
- Sharp scissors
- Utility knife blade
- Fine sandpaper and sanding block
- Round blending brush
- Detail brushes
- Water mister
- Acrylic paint *optional*
- Lint-free cloth
- Clear polyurethane
- Foam mini roller

1. Prepare the cabinet as usual by cleaning using degreaser and a kitchen sponge, and then removing all the hardware. On this project, the hardware was particularly worn so I kept it all together in a safe place to clean up later. (See Chapter 3 for cleaning hardware.)

2. Check over your piece for any necessary repairs such as filling and gluing. The foot on this tallboy had come loose, so I used some wood glue and attached the broken piece back in place **(a)**, leaving it to dry fully; use clamps or masking tape to hold the pieces tightly in position if needed.

3. Next, scuff sand the surface. With this design, most of the cabinet will be covered in wallpaper, so only light sanding is required to create a key for the paint to stick to. I used an electrical orbital sander for this step **(b)**; however, you can also scuff sand by hand if you do not have one of these available to you. (See Chapter 3 for sanding.) Once you have sanded all the surfaces lightly, rub everything down using a tack cloth.

4. Remove any doors using the appropriate screwdriver. Hinges will often need a proper clean-up on a piece this old, and this can only be done properly once removed; but I always feel it's worth it to create a neater look at the end! It also allows easier access to the interior for cleaning and refinishing.

5. Next, decide on a paint colour. Try to choose a base colour that matches in with the wallpaper you have chosen to use, as this will help it to blend in with the rest of the piece. Then load up your roller evenly and apply an even coat of chalk-based paint to the cabinet; I tend to work one side at a time, rolling in long vertical uniform strokes **(c)**.

6. To make a start with the wallpaper, first check how it fits onto your piece of furniture by holding it up and working out where you would like the pattern to sit **(d)**. I was lucky here, as I didn't need to do any measuring and could do it by eye. However, depending on the dimensions and design of the piece you are working on, you may need to measure and create a central line to work from to ensure your pattern is evenly placed.

7. Apply a layer of PVA glue with a flat brush to the areas you want to decoupage. I suggest working in sections, so that the glue doesn't dry out too quickly, applying plenty of glue around the edges in particular to prevent the paper lifting up.

8. Place the paper in position gently and, once straight, smooth down using either your hand **(e)** or a squeegee tool to get rid of any bubbles.

9. I recommend trimming down most of the excess wallpaper as you go along, using a sharp pair of scissors and leaving a slight overhang. Then, leave overnight to dry fully.

10. Once dry, use a sharp razor blade held at an angle to trim away the excess paper **(f)**; this will create a nice clean cut and avoid any tearing. When all the paper is trimmed away neatly, reattach the cabinet doors. Finally, check the edges of the paper for any signs of lifting and glue down with more PVA if necessary.

    You could leave your project here if you like the look. However, to create a more painterly feel and to achieve the effect of the pattern wrapping around the project we are going to paint over the paper. Yes, you read that correctly!

11. To begin this stage, lightly sand the surface of the wallpaper with fine sandpaper and a sanding block **(g)**. The aim is only to rough up the surface a tiny bit, making it a little more absorbent for paint, but also to create a slightly more aged look. Pass the sanding block over the surface very gently, perhaps applying a little more pressure towards the edges of the piece to neaten and distress them, until you are happy with it. Wipe away any dust created with a tack cloth.

12. Next it is time to blend in the wallpaper more with the frame and also give it a hand-painted look, so again, select a colour palette that will match in with your chosen paper. I am using mostly chalk paint here as before with a touch of acrylics, but feel free to experiment with what you have on hand. Then pick out the darkest or most prominent colour of your palette and use a round blending brush to apply the paint very sparingly to the piece. Create shaded areas by picking out the edges **(h)**, leaving the middle sections with no paint on them so there is a contrast of dark and light.

13. Use a water mister on the painted area, spraying a minimal amount of moisture onto the surface, which will cause the paint to thin a little; this will allow you to blend and shade the colour out with your blending brush to create a subtle faded and aged effect **(i)**.

TIP

Using a wallpaper design with an all-over pattern is a good idea for beginners. It means that the design will always be balanced across the piece and you won't need to worry about the placement so much.

BETTER THAN NEW

14. Add more base colours to help the paper blend into the paintwork. Of course this will depend on the wallpaper design you have decided on; for this leopard-print design I am using green. Use a combination of your blending brush and a kitchen sponge here to help blend the two colours into each other **(j)**.

15. Now begin to add in details using a smaller detail brush. I am looking to mimic the pattern that is already there, adding back in the definition to create an all-over hand-painted look **(k)**. I use paler colours such as mint green to create some highlights, which will make the pattern pop again.

16. Continue to use the water mister sparingly to blur the edges of your paintwork, with a lint-free cloth or kitchen sponge on hand to blot away any drips as you go, as this will soften the whole effect.

17. Extend the design in the same way all around the corners of the cabinet, the sides and onto detailed features such as the feet and even the hardware if desired, to create a seamless look; carry on repeating the earlier steps until you are happy.

18. Once the paint is fully dry, use fine sandpaper on an angle, moving it away from the wallpaper to smooth off all the edges. This will prevent the paper from lifting and make everything look neat and tidy.

19. As we are using mostly chalk-based paint and wallpaper, the whole cabinet will need to be sealed at the end to protect the paper and the paintwork. Use clear polyurethane with a foam roller to protect every surface. (See Chapter 3 for sealing.)

20. Finally, use a mini screwdriver or a bradawl to carefully poke a hole through the wallpaper on the reverse of the cabinet door, and reattach all the hardware **(l)**.

TIP

Search for clues about your item's provenance by looking for maker's marks. These will often be found on the back of a piece or inside drawers. I discovered that this piece was made by British Maker Harris Lebus and also carried the CC41 Utility mark, which was applied to furniture made in Britain during and just after the Second World War.

project 6
mint geometric

before

I found this chest of drawers hanging around on an online auction site looking desperate for a friend. It went for very little money, as I think the fact that it was a big rescue mission put a lot of people off, and the thought did cross my mind to avoid it altogether. But mid-century furniture is becoming much more sought after nowadays, so I knew that by the end of the transformation someone would fall in love with it, even though it seemed unlikely at first. The straight lines were a perfect blank canvas and personally I enjoyed playing around with textures on this one and adding details to replace the character that had been lost from its early days. Funny story, though, this chest of drawers was so cheap due to its poor condition that I actually paid out more for the replacement handles, and I can't get my head around that. It shows two things: if you are prepared to take on some work, then you can really find a good deal; but also that vintage handles are very sought after, so try to hold on to them when you can!

SELECT MATERIALS

- Painter's masking tape
- Water based primer
- Eggshell paint
- Water based paint (such as Emulsion or chalk based paint) for the whitewash
- Short pile mini roller & tray
- Medium pile mini roller
- Flat brush
- PVA glue
- Textured wallpaper (anaglypta)
- Sharp scissors
- Utility knife blade
- Kitchen sponge
- Lint-free cloth
- Wood oil
- Clear polyurethane
- Foam mini roller

1. First, I removed the handles **(a)**. These were not original and didn't have a lot of age to them; I was able to unscrew each one carefully with my hands; however, use a screwdriver if needed. Keep the handles in case you can reuse them on another project, but I will look for some vintage replacements a little more in keeping with the style of this piece a bit later on.

2. Strip down the old painted finish using a carbide scraper **(b)**. Approach the edges carefully with the blade, reducing the pressure ever so slightly and going slowly with the grain to prevent catching and lifting up the mid-century veneer.

3. I used a heat gun (wearing heat-resistant gloves) and a small wire brush to loosen the last bits of paint from intricate areas such as trim and bevelled edges that couldn't be reached with the scraper **(c)**. (See Chapter 3 for using a heat gun.)

4. Begin to sand the frame. On this occasion, I turned the drawers upside down and sanded the legs **(d)**; these turned out to be solid wood, so I used a triangular attachment on my orbital sander to get tight into the corners (or you could use a sanding block or a mouse sander instead, as mentioned in Chapter 3) The newly revealed natural wood base makes a beautiful contrast to the paintwork above.

5. If you decide to keep any natural wood areas, you may want to give each surface a final sand by hand to get that super-smooth finish. (Follow the instructions in Project 13). Then wipe down every surface with a tack cloth to remove any dust, and use painter's masking tape to block out the areas you don't want to get paint on.

6. Paint the frame and drawers using a short pile mini roller and water based primer, leaving the legs unpainted (optional). I also left the top drawer unprimed at this stage because I wanted to do something different with it in the later steps.

7. Once the primer is dry, use the same painting technique to apply your chosen colour to the frame **(e)**. I used a mint green eggshell, and applied as many coats as required for good coverage, fine sanding between coats to get a super-smooth finish. Once dry, check that the drawers are all in the right compartments; or if it's easier to work with them on the floor, go for it; just double check they are in the right order, and the correct way up before you start to decoupage.

8. With this particular project, first I would recommend considering where all the handles are going to sit; place the paper on your piece, making sure the pattern looks relatively balanced on either side of the hardware; of course it all depends on the wallpaper pattern you are using, but it's worth considering before you commit to sticking anything down!

9. Then apply PVA glue to the surface of the first drawer you want to cover with wallpaper using a flat paintbrush and follow Steps 6–9 from Project 5 to apply to the surface. When decoupaging drawers, be sure to continue the pattern so that it matches seamlessly from one piece to the next. To do this I prefer to cut the paper to shape where it will need to match the next drawer as I go along; I'd advise pressing the paper down onto the glue quite hard to create a good crease line **(f)**, and then cutting along carefully with sharp scissors where the pattern needs to continue while wet. Repeat this step until all the drawers are covered.

DECOUPAGE

10. Leave to dry overnight, then tidy up any rough edges using a utility knife blade, holding it at an angle to cut away any excess paper and create a much neater line **(g)**. As the textured paper we are using is quite thick, I also use a fine sandpaper and a sanding block lightly against the edge, again held at an angle to smooth away any imperfections.

11. While this was drying I turned my attention to the top drawer, the one I didn't paint. I could have oiled it and left it as natural wood to add character to the piece; however, I chose to use a whitewash. Mix water with your chosen paint (it can be anything water based, such as emulsion or chalk-based paint) until you get a single cream consistency (as in Project 2), then apply this mixture with a sponge onto the sanded drawer **(h)**. Use even downward strokes, going with the grain, rubbing away any excess paint using a dry lint-free cloth to create a washed effect which we will seal later.

12. When all the papered areas are fully dry, we can paint them. I opted for a two-tone look on this project, so decided to use a paler version of the green I used on the frame. I used a medium pile roller so that the slightly longer pile would get into the grooves of the textured paper **(i)**.

13. Peel away the painter's masking tape to reveal the areas of natural wood, then use wood oil to seal these areas and the legs. I used a lint-free cloth and some white wood oil because I wanted to achieve a natural look **(j)**. (See Chapter 3 for oiling wood.) However, you could also seal with another top coat such as wax or polyurethane if preferred.

14. Now protect the surface of all the drawer fronts with clear polyurethane using a foam roller. (See Chapter 3 for advice on sealing.) For this project apply multiple coats of clear polyurethane to seal the paper properly and achieve a really robust and hard wearing finish.

15. Lastly, add your choice of hardware. I had some vintage handles which I had planned to use for a previous project **(k)**. The style and age were perfectly suited to a set of drawers like this, making the design look authentic, but I added a contemporary twist by cleaning them up and adding black detailing for the extra wow factor. (See Project 11 for painting hardware.)

chapter 6

furniture art

I can't help but see furniture as a canvas, as it is possible to paint anything with the right refinishing skills, and an old chest of drawers can be so much more than just a place to put your socks. Instead, it could be a really beautiful place to put your socks, both functional and aesthetically pleasing, but also personal. As a furniture artist, I have definitely noticed that our interior styles and tastes have become a little bit braver in recent years; we want our spaces to reflect our personality and unique style. This is probably why hand painting art onto furniture has enjoyed a resurgence lately. Art on furniture is not a new concept; after all, as they say, no good idea is an entirely new idea. If you think back to folk art, for example, you would commonly see furniture or everyday objects being used as a canvas for creative expression. I feel as though you can always rely on decorative furniture to add a pop of personality to a space, in the same way that patterns on our clothing, community murals or the art we choose to put on our walls are forms of personal expression. In addition to this, brand new materials, with different paints and products continually being launched into the marketplace, encourage experimentation and a more playful approach to furniture design and have also led to the rise of furniture art. In this chapter we will look at just a few techniques and ideas you could try out to create a personal and truly bespoke design using hand-painted or drawn techniques. However, feel free to paint the Mona Lisa if that's your thing!

FURNITURE ART

project 7

hand-painted floral

before

When I first saw this vintage cupboard, I was attracted to its simplicity. At first glance it doesn't look much and the grey gloss paint finish leaves a lot to be desired, but I will always consider previously painted pieces of furniture. Yes, more work is involved, but the extra effort is worth it to keep these items in use for longer. On the positive side, the 1950s utility style with simple details really appealed to me; it was a great size and I was deliberately looking for a project with flat surfaces, as this always makes the perfect blank canvas. I typically choose to paint artwork on furniture that is either quite damaged or very plain in design, because a bespoke design can be just the thing to add the wow factor it so desperately needs. I will be using chalk-based paint on this project, so will keep the prep minimal, meaning I can get stuck straight into being creative. I am definitely thinking something floral because flowers are my thing – however, you could use any of the techniques shown to paint a design of your choosing so feel free to experiment!

SELECT MATERIALS

- Chalk-based paint (in colours of your choice)
- Chalk-based paint (White)
- Acrylics *optional*
- Flat brush or short pile mini roller
- Detail brushes in varying sizes
- Water soluble pastels or pencils
- Matt spray varnish
- Clear polyurethane
- Foam mini roller & tray

1. Since the piece had been painted a few times before, the doors would not close properly due to paint drips and build-up around the edges of the cupboard; it's a common problem for furniture of this time and I needed to take off the doors to fix it. However, on further investigation, the hinges were really caked up with paint and I couldn't even turn the screws to remove them, so first I applied paint stripper to each hinge with a small brush and left overnight.

2. After the paint had bubbled up, I took a fine wire brush and rubbed away the layers of old paint to reveal the metalware **(a)**. This allowed me to loosen the old screws and remove the hinges with a flat-head screwdriver. I set the hinges aside to clean up and reattach later. (See Chapter 3 for paint stripping and cleaning hardware.)

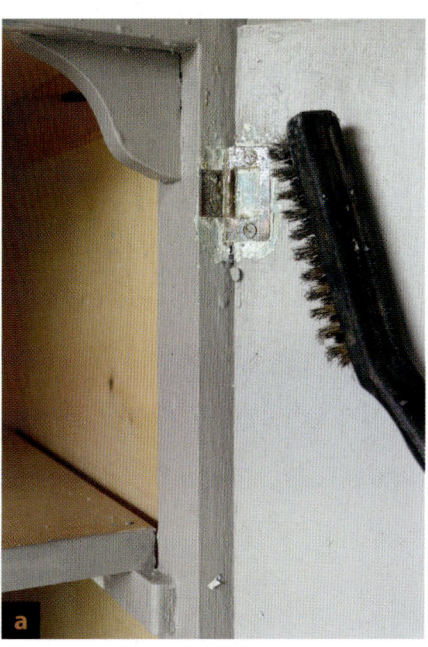

3. With the messy bit done, I scuff sanded the cupboard with an orbital sander, smoothing out the old paint. Since I was using chalk-based paint, prep wasn't strictly necessary but as the cupboard had been painted many times before, the process eliminated any raised areas such as drips, before painting. (See Chapter 3 for sanding.)

4. I gave the cupboard a good wipe down with a tack cloth to pick up any excess dust. The aim of this is to achieve quite a smooth and modern finish with the paintwork, so don't skip this step. I know the prep seems a lot on a previously painted piece, but it helps to get a better result at the end.

5. Then I masked off the interior and anything I didn't want to paint over, such as hardware, with painter's masking tape and finally I was ready to paint. I applied a bright pink chalk-based paint using a flat brush **(b)**, but a roller would also work well if preferred. (See Chapter 3 for painting.) Apply as many coats of paint as are needed, leaving drying time in between, until you are happy with the coverage.

6. Once they were fully dry, I reattached the now-clean hinges and added the doors back on. It may seem strange to do it in this order, but personally I find it easier to paint my design while everything is in place, so I can envisage how my hand-painted design will work across the whole piece.

7. I use a water soluble pastel to draw some very rough flower shapes onto the cabinet doors **(c)**. I personally prefer to draw in quite a large scale, covering the piece and going around the sides. Try to keep your hand quite flexible and stand a little bit away from your project to encourage more of a loose line. I suggest leaving roughly a third of empty or negative space against your design for contrast; it can really help a composition look striking. However, this is very much an organic process, and beauty is in the eye of the beholder, so plan your design as you feel.

8. Begin painting in the floral shapes with larger brushes **(d)**. I like to start with darker, more vivid shades, creating some energetic and loose marks with a large brush. (Remember the lines you have already drawn are just acting as a guide, so don't worry if you cover some of them or the design changes, as this is a very free way of working.) My painting style is very expressive, so I used loose shapes as a starting point but you can be more exact if you want to.

9. Next, stating the obvious… add more colours! There are no set rules, but to inspire you to make a start, I tend to go for a contrasting colour (for example, the orange **[e, f]**) at this stage alongside different versions

of the colour I began with; so here I used navy blue and a teal blue. Fill in the shapes as you see fit, adding shapes and loose lines to form the base of the flowers. Experiment with different sizes and shapes of brush; the varied brushstrokes add interest, working well to create depth in your paintwork.

10. Try adding a tiny bit of white to mix paler versions of the same colour; this works well straight onto the piece to create shaded areas and achieves a three-dimensional look. As you continue to work on your design, if you make a mistake, don't worry at all. The beauty of chalk-based paint means it will wipe away easily with a damp cloth and you can make adjustments as you go along, or just paint over it!

11. Next, I began to draw back in some outlines using the water soluble pastels again **(g)**. Feel free to experiment with different colours here, and keep quite a loose feel; this will help to add more form to the flowers as you go along. You can even begin to add extra details, such as stems and leaves around the edges, if you think the design needs it.

12. Once the first few layers are completely dry, I then like to use fine detail brushes, thinning the paint with water to make it glide on the surface, which makes it easier to create finer, flowing lines – it makes such a difference. Paint loose outlines around the floral shapes using interesting marks and squiggles in contrasting colours to make things stand out. Here I used a bright green, which really pops **(h)**.

13. Once everything has dried again, begin to repaint around your artwork in your chosen background colour, cutting into all of the shapes with a smaller detail brush **(i)**. This helps to redefine each floral or stem shape, adding extra definition and your design will come to life.

14. For the final flourish, I drew again onto my design, adding details and dynamic lines with the water soluble pastels **(j)**. These created a sense of movement and a graphic feel to the final design. Don't think about the placement too much, as this will create more of an expressive feel to your artwork. (Keep in mind that you can use the pastels at any time during the painting process on wet or dry paint to create different effects.)

15. When you are completely finished, as part of the sealing process, apply to your floral design an even layer of spray varnish **(k)**. Keep in mind that water soluble pastels will smudge when you brush or roll anything wet on the surface so spray sealing is necessary first to avoid smudging. When you come to seal the piece fully later on, it will keep your artwork and all the lines you have drawn in intact. (See Project 11 Spray Painting Handles.)

16. Once the spray varnished areas have fully dried, seal the whole piece using clear polyurethane with a foam mini roller; I like to apply a good three to four coats here to properly seal in the design and fine sanding in between coats. (See Chapter 3 for sealing.)

TIP

Take photographs of your work as you go along. This really helps to gain perspective on whether the design is working or not, and can help with envisioning what to do next.
Use a sketchbook to build confidence with your design. Take time experimenting with different shapes, mark making and colour schemes before you take the plunge and paint onto a piece of furniture.

project 8

abstract landscape

before

When I found this set of drawers in a vintage shop amongst second-hand clothes and old knick-knacks I fell in love with the curvy shape and 1950s brass details. We were on a family holiday at the time but I just couldn't leave this behind, so managed to squeeze it in the car amongst all the luggage and children! Clearly, this mid-century chest of drawers had already been revamped at some stage in its life, but now it was looking very tired and in need of attention again. The best thing about refinishing furniture, though, is that we never have to get rid of anything; even when the condition is poor or the style factor lacking, potential is everywhere. On the first look, I didn't like the wood-effect vinyl or the pine bun feet which were clearly a late addition to this retro piece. What I did see, however, was the possibility of a huge transformation, which is always exciting; and mid-century furniture in particular works really well with abstract artwork because of the cool shapes, sleek lines and flat surfaces, so this is a perfect canvas. For your project, I'd definitely recommend keeping or sourcing interesting hardware which will really pop out within an abstract composition.

SELECT MATERIALS

- Short pile mini roller & tray
- Multi-surface primer
- Eggshell paint (for the frame)
- Cordless drill & small wood drill bit
- Vintage legs x4
- Painter's masking tape
- Eggshell or chalk-based paint (for the design)
- Variety of paintbrushes in different widths (flat brushes work well but there are no set rules)
- Water mister
- Lint-free cloths

For this project I used eggshell paint with a built-in topcoat. However, chalk-based paints would also work well for this abstract technique. If using, remember that your piece will require sealing afterwards. (See Chapter 3 for sealing.)

1. Remove the handles using the correct size screwdriver and put these aside **(a)**. Mine were an original retro shape made from brass, so I was confident they would look the star of the show once cleaned up. (See Chapter 3 for cleaning hardware.) I also carefully removed the brass-coloured edging sitting in a recess around the top of the chest to make the frame easier to paint, but don't worry – I will put it back later, as caring for original details can really make your piece stand out from the crowd!

2. To remove the vinyl I used a heat gun (wear heat-resistant gloves) to loosen the glue underneath ever so slightly. (See Chapter 3 for using a heat gun.) Keep in mind that vinyl is a type of plastic and can melt, so for this project keep the heat gun on a low heat setting, being careful not to hold it too close to the surface; then use a stripping knife to peel away as much of the vinyl covering as you can **(b)**.

3. Next, I turned the chest upside down to unscrew the old pine legs from the base **(c)**. I felt these weren't right for the style of the piece, so I put them aside to use on a different project.

4. With filling or repairs done (see Chapter 3 for wood filling), I sanded down the curved surface of the frame with sandpaper and a sanding block to remove any small bits of residue or glue left from the stripping process. (See Chapter 3 for sanding.) For this project I paid particular attention to the top of the chest, as this was covered in shiny laminate and needed to be sanded well, ideally with an orbital sander, before any painting could take place **(d)**.

5. Fully prepped, I began to prime the frame with a mini roller. (See Chapter 3 for painting.) Remember that if you are going to paint the frame a darker colour as I did, be sure to use a grey primer to aid paint coverage later on. I also used a multi-surface primer to cover the laminate surfaces on this project.

6. Once the multi surface primer had fully dried, I decided to paint just the frame in a dark grey eggshell, creating a smooth, contemporary finish **(e)**. (See Chapter 3 for painting.) Apply as many coats as required to achieve full coverage, leaving drying time in between.

7. When the paint had fully cured, I turned the frame upside down and began to attach new legs to the base. I found a great set of vintage wooden legs online, which were more in keeping with the original character of the piece and raised the chest off the floor making it seem more in proportion. I used a cordless drill to make small pilot holes first **(f)**, making it easier to insert the screws, before screwing everything securely into place with a screwdriver.

I then stood the chest of drawers back up the right way with the drawers inside. This is because I prefer to paint the drawers upright and in situ; however, you can remove them if you prefer.

8. I begin to mask out the frame, using low-tack painter's masking tape and making sure to press it down firmly **(g)**; this is to prevent any bleed through (see page 48).

9. To begin painting the abstract design, collect together a good selection of brushes. Try to use brushes of varying widths and styles to create interest; the more you have the more interesting your design will be, but honestly there are no rules here, anything goes! Personally I love flat brushes for this technique, especially with wider bristles.

10. I used a really large flat brush to apply a paler colour in a loose fashion across the drawer fronts, creating a base layer **(h)**. The idea is to get some natural-looking strokes, so don't think too much about this part and keep your movements quite loose; make sure to leave some of the paint underneath showing through.

11. At this stage I began to add a little more colour, applying blush pink to add interest **(i)**. Again, there are no set rules as to what colour you use but I tend to use a mid-tone colour at this point – something between your darkest and lightest colours (in this example grey and white) – using a similar brush to before but smaller in width. This is so that I can begin to build up a little more definition in the paintwork.

12. Next, use a water mister to wet the surface and dilute the paint where you feel it needs it **(j)**; this can soften hard edges and create some interesting marks. If you get drips, this is absolutely fine, but you may prefer to blot out some areas using a lint-free cloth dabbed onto the surface **(k)**; this will soften hard lines where desired.

BETTER THAN NEW

14. When this layer is completely dry, use a larger flat brush to apply thinned-down paint in a lighter colour over the top of everything **(l)**, keeping movement in your brushstrokes and leaving some colour showing from underneath as before. This will do a good job of knocking some of the more vibrant areas back, creating a sense of background and foreground.

15. Once this is dry, peel away the masking tape, revealing your finished artwork **(m)**. This bit always feels very exciting and you will see the abstract painting suddenly come together, framed by the dark outer edge of the drawers. I like to think of it as a picture frame.

16. Finally, I applied the cleaned-up original brass trim **(n)** and reattached the handles. These have been stripped back to brass **(o)**. (See Chapter 3 for cleaning hardware.) Wow, sometimes handles are the icing on the cake. I am so pleased with how these look!

TIP

Changing the legs on furniture can really elevate the look of your final design. For example, going for a different style or altering the height of a piece of furniture will really modernise the look. Try searching for vintage legs on eBay to add character and save on buying new.

Abstract art is very subjective, so experiment with layers and don't worry too much if it doesn't go to plan. Anything you paint is just another layer to work with, adding depth and dimension to your work. Just repeat, repeat, repeat until you like what you see!

project 9
doodle drawers

before

One of the great things about upcyling furniture for a living is that every so often you get given a piece for free! It's amazing the number of discarded pieces I have been offered over the years because, let's face it, it's hard to find the time sometimes, isn't it, and also the space? This set of drawers, though, was given to me by my mum. It had been stored in her garage for years, and there was a layer of dust to prove it, but I was very happy when she said I could take this off her hands – in fact I may even have used a bit of gentle persuasion! The condition was fine, apart from the missing handle, but other than that, this was another blank canvas to create something special with; and one of the things I loved doing as a child was doodling! For me doodling is about filling the page with pattern and interesting shapes. Do you remember sitting bored at school and doodling all over the page just to escape the boredom in maths? It's a therapeutic process and I love the way it makes you unwind and relax – my children and I have always loved using paint pens to create with at home so I'm looking forward to showing you this one.

SELECT MATERIALS

- Painter's masking tape
- Water based Primer
- Gesso primer *optional*
- Short pile mini roller & tray
- Eggshell paint (for the frame)
- Flat brush
- Sketchbook
- Detail brushes in varying sizes
- Acrylic paints or tester pots
- 5mm acrylic paint pens
- Clear polyurethane
- Mini foam roller & tray
- Cordless drill & wood drill bit
- Vintage handles

1. First clean the piece down with a degreaser and a lint-free cloth. On this occasion the chest was very dusty from living in the garage for so long, but the condition was good. One of the issues, though, was a missing handle which would need to be replaced, so I removed the old handles and set them aside.

2. Make any repairs required. (See Chapter 3 for repairing.) Then, use an orbital sander to very lightly pass across the larger surface areas to give the surface a key.

3. Use fine sandpaper to rub carefully along all the edges of the drawers and frame, holding the sandpaper at a slight angle. This will create an even smoother finish, but is also a preventative measure after the process of sanding, to stop any veneer pulling up at the edge; then wipe down your project with a tack cloth to remove dust.

TIP

If you are struggling with a colour scheme, try going to your wardrobe and looking at your favourite clothes. Find interesting patterns and colour combos and pick out the colours for your project.

TIP

Experiment with a bright contrasting colour on the base or legs of your furniture project to suit your colour scheme. Or, for a more vintage look, you could strip the legs back to natural wood following the steps in Chapter 3.

4. The base on this piece was removable, which is often the case with mid-century furniture, so I decided to remove it before painting, using a screwdriver **(a)**. This is not always necessary but I do find it a lot easier to prep and paint once the base has been removed.

5. If the edges of your drawers look a bit messy, use painter's masking tape to square them off, pressing it down really firmly. I used a water based primer with a mini short pile roller to prime the whole unit, including the legs and also the masked-out edges of the drawers **(b)**.

6. Turn the roller vertically to paint the side of the drawers, smoothing out any drips where paint could have built up on the edges. I suggest a couple of coats of primer, then wait until everything is fully dry.

7. The panels in the middle will be quite brightly decorated, so for the frame surrounding them, I chose a neutral peach eggshell and began to paint the base first. The plan was for the coloured drawers to pop out and make a statement by contrasting with the neutral frame.

8. Once the base was dry, I used a screwdriver to reattach it securely to the rest of the piece. Having the drawers raised up on the legs would make everything else easier to paint.

9. With the drawers now turned the right way up, I turned my attention to the frame, painting it the same colour as the legs **(c)**. I also painted the edges of the drawers with peach eggshell where I had masked them off previously, including the tops.

10. I recommend doing most of the painting work using your roller. However, you may also need a flat brush on hand to paint any of the small details. Leave everything to dry fully. I would recommend about two to three coats of eggshell paint to achieve full coverage.

11. Once fully dry, remove the painter's masking tape from the edge of the drawers to reveal a crisp, neat line. Place a new piece of masking tape all around the painted edge of the drawers, to protect from overspill, and press down securely.

12. Next, although I had already prepared the frame and drawers with a regular DIY primer, I applied an extra layer of white gesso to the drawers **(d)**. This is a product I used when I was a canvas artist, and it is really good, providing a little more tooth for acrylic paints to grip onto. I find the regular DIY primers can sometimes be a little slippery, but gesso is a thicker consistency, helping the acrylic paint to penetrate the surface a lot better; this means the colours will look more intense and vibrant.

13. While the gesso layer was drying, I collected together a selection of acrylic paints and acrylic paint pens – you could use tester pots too if you wanted. I also gathered some detail brushes to apply the paint and a little cup of water to wash my brush when required, with a lint-free cloth to the side to clean off any excess water.

14. For this type of project, I use a sketchbook to draw out some rough doodle patterns using all the paints, and practise making different patterns such as dots, squiggles, zig zags, lines and circles **(e)**. I just keep drawing until the pages get completely full. This is a great way to experiment with mark making and colour combinations before you commit to painting it on the piece.

15. At this stage you may find it easier to remove the drawers from the chest, working with them on a flat surface. (However, for the purposes of demonstration in this book I have placed them back into the chest, as it is easier to photograph the process.) With my sketchbook images on hand as inspiration, I began to paint a thicker, slightly wavy line, going from one side of the drawers to another. This whole process is quite organic, so do what you feel in terms of design – but a line across the middle is a good place to start.

16. Then I continued to add more lines in the same colour to balance out the line in the middle **(f)**. I was trying to make sure I had a little of the navy blue across the whole composition at first, in order to make the whole thing balanced. Go wild with the shape of your lines too and try to make each one a little different.

17. To get a smooth edge to your lines, dab your brush in a tiny bit of water, or try adding a little water to the paint to help it glide across the surface. Hold your brush lower down and at an angle to get more control and definition.

18. Next, I started with a second colour, adding in a large oval shape to add some interest to the pattern **(g)**, but keeping in mind that each time I add a colour, it needs to be repeated across the whole piece in some form or another. Make sure to mix up the shapes you paint as you move across the drawers; I find it an effective way of working and this technique will help you to form a pattern quite quickly.

19. Repeat this process again and again, each time using a different colour and varying the larger shapes. For example, next I drew an 's' wiggle shape in neon pink **(h)**.

FURNITURE ART

20. Once you have done this with around eight to ten different colours, move on to acrylic paint pens to fill in some of the gaps. Give them a good shake, and press onto a test piece of paper to get the ink flowing. Then begin to add in dots or lines, even little squiggles where there is empty space, again alternating between colours as shown **(i)**.

21. When you are happy with the design, fill in the background colour using a contrasting colour **(j)**. Choose a shade that you haven't already used when making the pattern to make sure each shape stands out; and cut into each shape using a detail brush until the whole background is filled in. You may be wondering why I didn't paint the background colour first and then paint on top? This is because my background was quite a strong blue which would have affected the vibrancy of the paint colours I was using on top; for example, the neon colours would not have shown up on a dark background in the same way. So as I wanted really colour-popping shades, I used the white gesso first.

22. When the background has had a couple of coats and is dry, feel free to go back in and make any final amendments to the shapes with your detail brushes – or acrylic paint pens are the perfect tool for this giving you extra precision – then leave the design to dry fully.

23. Seal the whole surface using clear polyurethane and a foam roller **(k)**. (See Chapter 3 for sealing.) This will protect your design from wear and tear and make it practical for daily use.

24. Lastly, add on your new handles **(l)**. I had to drill a larger hole with a cordless drill, for the new hardware which I rescued from an old chest of drawers and had been saving for a rainy day. They look perfect – super happy with this one!

chapter 7

alternative techniques

At this stage in the book we have learned how to use paint and paper to revitalise a piece; and the more familiar materials will always have an extremely important role to play in most furniture projects because they are easily accessible to us. However, in this chapter I want to look at the variety of innovative materials we can also use to refresh old items. I love to paint furniture, but from a design point of view I think there's even more potential when we start to consider using alternative materials to revamp our projects; it can create a completely different look and opens up a world of possibilities in design. I have only just scratched the surface with these projects and there are many other options – and I hope, in future, more sustainable ones too – but hopefully you will leave this section in the book feeling inspired to try something a little different. Being innovative and forward thinking in this way will continue to keep furniture refinishing and upcycling relevant to modern day living in the future, and that is super important!

ALTERNATIVE TECHNIQUES

project 10

blue mirror

Glass cabinets are everywhere and I really like to see them used in bathrooms for lotions or potions or, better still, utilised as drinks cabinets for a cheeky cocktail when the mood is right! This cabinet, though… well let's just say the lady in the shop looked at me funny when I asked if I could buy it. It had seen better days but it was so unique; and the feature that really attracted me, despite the condition, was the unusual beading on the front, as well as, of course, all the glass. Glass can be overlooked and I wanted to see if I could make it the standout feature, but the original panes were really old and flimsy; so I decided to replace with modern reeded panels which are a lot stronger and would add more strength to the piece. This process is quite in depth and the materials I have used are not cheap; however, I wanted to show you what was possible for a high-end and contemporary look. If preferred, use just one of these ideas to revamp your project or consider reeded vinyl as an alternative to the glass.

before

Instead of acrylic use wallpaper, or paint the back of the cabinet a contrasting colour instead.

Just to mention, at first I had the idea to strip the wood on this piece but I decided half way through that painting the wood would look better. So don't feel you need to strip your piece back as much as I did – a quick scuff sand will be perfectly fine.

SELECT MATERIALS

- Stripping knife
- Tack hammer
- Safety goggles
- Protective gloves
- Pliers
- Clear primer
- Short pile mini roller & tray
- Eggshell paint
- Small paintbrush
- Tape measure
- Reeded glass (cut to size)
- Clear contact glue
- Retaining nails
- Nail punch
- Pine trim
- Mitre cutter
- Acrylic sheet (cut to size)
- Instant grab adhesive
- Sealant gun

1. To get started I removed the plinth on the top to create a more contemporary silhouette **(a)**; it's surprising what a difference this trick makes to the look of a finished piece, and I wanted things to look more streamlined and modern. In this case the spare beading on the plinth will come in useful in Step 6. Luckily the plinth pretty much fell off for me, but if you are struggling to remove this kind of feature, first check for screws, then try a flat scraping tool and a hammer or similar to get underneath the wood and prise up gently. Fill any old holes if necessary, using epoxy wood filler. (See Chapter 3 for wood filling.)

115

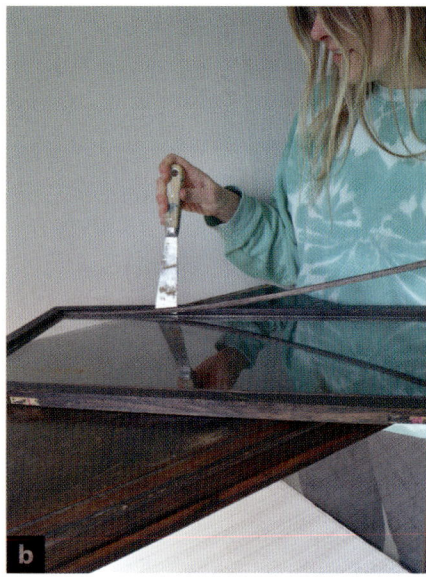

2. Then remove the doors and hardware such as hinges with a screwdriver. As always, keep your hardware safe for cleaning later as hinges are difficult to replace. (See Chapter 3 for cleaning hardware.) I also removed the shelving inside, giving me better access to the back of the cabinet. For the next part you will need to wear safety goggles. I used a flat scraping tool such as a stripping knife, which allowed me to prise the beading away without damaging the trim or the glass **(b)**. Hold the tool flat against the frame and tap it very gently, pushing into the gaps behind the beading until you get any kind of movement. It's very trial and error but the key is to just be gentle and patient. Where you get some movement, focus on that spot and with a bit of perseverance you will gradually be able to prise the beading away from the frame. Try not to snap the wooden beading by bending it too much or going too quickly, as there may be retaining nails keeping it in place. If so, place your tool behind where the retaining nails sit, making it easier to prise the trim away without snapping it. That said, though, if you do break some beading, don't worry, we can replace it in the later steps!

   Note: Glass is often kept in place using either putty or wooden beading; I was removing wooden beading, which I would say is slightly easier. When removing putty, use a chopping knife instead.

3. If by the end of this process you still find any retaining nails left in the frame, or in the beading itself, carefully remove these with pliers. We will use new nails to secure so there is no need to keep the old ones, but keep as much original beading as possible to save on waste.

4. Using protective gloves, I continued to remove all panes of old glass very carefully on all sides until I was left with just the wooden frame. Your project will feel a bit rickety at this stage but when we put the new thicker glass in, it will strengthen back up again.

5. Next, strip the old covering from the back of the cabinet and from the shelves. For this project, I used a spray mister filled with warm water to saturate the surface; be sure to spray and leave to soak into the paper or fabric for five to ten minutes, making it easier to remove. Use your scraping tool until all of the paper is gone **(c)**. (You could also use a heat gun on a low setting for this step.)

6. It's a good time to check if anything needs repair at this stage. For this piece, I noticed that some of the beading was missing, so I reused a small piece taken from the top panel I had removed earlier, to replace the broken section on the leg **(d)**. I used wood glue and then masking tape to secure back in place.

7. Then lightly sand down the frame and doors, using a tack cloth afterwards to collect the sanding dust. You can then prime if necessary – for this cabinet I used a clear primer. (See Chapter 3 for sanding and priming.)

8. Apply your chosen paint colour with a short pile mini roller **(e)**. I chose a dark navy blue eggshell and painted the whole cabinet including the door frames, beading and the shelving. However, leave the back unpainted if using acrylic sheet to cover as in the later steps. (See Chapter 3 for painting.)

ALTERNATIVE TECHNIQUES

9. You may also find it useful to have a small paintbrush to paint the intricate details on a cabinet like this, such as the recess where the glass will sit; and to paint the beading strips removed in the earlier steps **(f)**. Keep in mind to paint all of these components fully, even on the reverse, as unpainted edges will show through the glass when it gets fixed back into place.

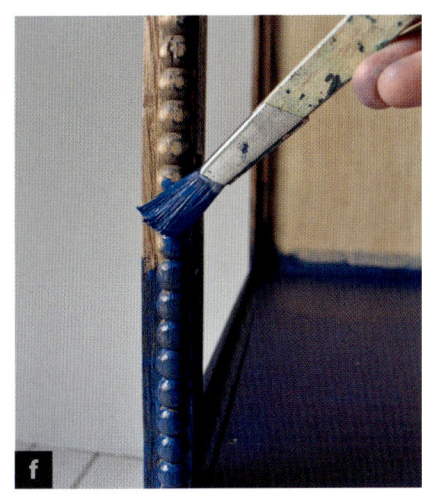

10. Next, I measured inside the recess where the new glass would sit. Be as accurate as you can with your measurements here, making sure the tape measure is straight and held tight into the recess both vertically and horizontally to get the true dimensions. The materials we are using in this project are cut to size and very hard to trim down at a later stage without the right machinery, so I usually write down two millimetres less than the actual measurement to be safe as this will make doubly sure the glass fits. Keep in mind we are using beading to secure in place, so you have a little bit of space to play with on the edges; but it's best to measure well as vintage furniture comes in all shapes and sizes and can often not be straight. I measure in the middle of the recess and at both ends of it, taking the smallest measurement to work from. As they say measure twice, cut once!

11. Continue to measure the back of the cabinet for the acrylic mirrored back panel. (Please see Resources for information on where to order glass and acrylic; however, you should be able to find reputable suppliers online or in your local area.)

12. Now it is time to fit the reeded glass into place. To prevent the glass from rattling I use a few dabs of clear contact glue around the recess of the frame, applying a minimal amount to prevent any spillage onto the glass **(g)**.

13. Then, using protective gloves, carefully press the glass panels into place against the glue **(h)**.

14. Secure the glass by fixing the wooden beading back into place using small retaining nails and a tack hammer, making sure that the glass is properly pushed against the frame as you fix in each piece **(i)**. I would recommend using the previous nail holes to make this process easier, but if this isn't possible use a nail punch to make a hole beforehand.

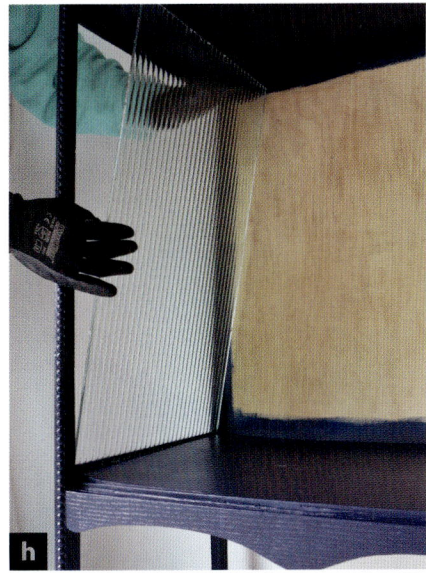
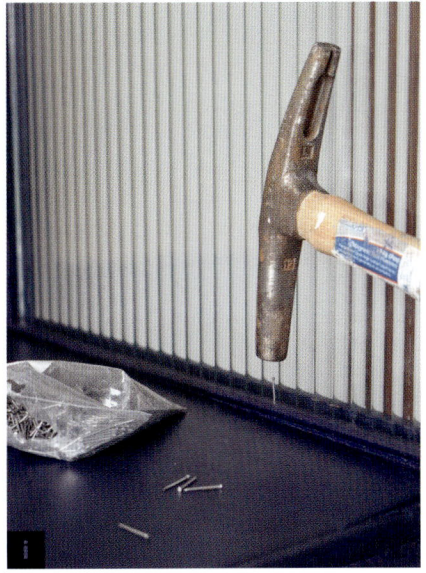

15. (Optional) If you need to replace any broken beading, use a thin pine wood trim, and cut to size using a mitre cutter **(j)**. This is so simple to use and will cut perfect mitred angles with ease. Then paint as in Step 9, and attach the trim as before.

16. Lastly I attach the acrylic mirrored panel to the back of the cabinet using a thick instant-grab adhesive which will hold the panel in place upon contact. Apply the sealant slightly in from the edges to prevent it squelching out as you press down **(k)**. For this I use a sealant gun.

17. Gently place the pre-cut panel in place and, once set, peel back the clear protective film **(l)**. Feel free to secure the back panel with beading the same way you did with the reeded glass panels if desired to create a nice neat finish.

18. Finally, add the shelf back in and reattach the doors and your hardware. I managed to find an old handle that suited this cabinet perfectly, which has been glammed up a little with gilding wax as a finishing touch.

ADDING VINTAGE HARDWARE

I took a dislike to the handle already on this drinks cabinet which I didn't feel was original and looked a little out of place. It's just a question of personal taste but I felt that changing this to something different would look better, and luckily I have a big box of second-hand hardware which I keep handy, full of interesting bits collected from vintage shops, fairs and car boot sales! Incredibly I found the perfect art deco handle which fitted perfectly, but just needed a tiny spruce up, so here's what I did.

YOU WILL NEED

Vintage handle
Metal polish
Kitchen sponge
Fine wire wool
Metallic gilding wax
Detail brush
Lint-free cloth
Screwdriver

a

1. Locate a beautiful handle from your stash if you have one and check it fits first!

2. Clean the handle with a metal polish and a kitchen sponge, or fine wire wool on its own to remove any rust or debris.

3. Add metallic gilding wax with a detail brush **(a)**.

4. Buff to a sheen with a lint-free cloth.

5. Attach with a screwdriver and that's it! (See other information on hardware in Chapter 3.)

TIP

This style of cabinet will often have a paper or fabric backing, so invest in a wallpaper stripper. It's a handy tool to have which will help to steam away the old coverings speedily and with ease.

ALTERNATIVE TECHNIQUES

project 11

neon cork

before

This mid-century miniature sideboard was listed on a second-hand marketplace, and I thought it was the perfect size for modern living. My first thoughts were perhaps to use it as a contemporary TV stand, as most of us need a functional piece of furniture like this at home, but I prefer mine with a bit more flair!

On closer inspection, it was made from particle board, a much trickier surface to paint, but this was easy to overlook as the dinky little size of this piece, the retro tapered legs and the original metallic handles got me quite excited! There was also some slight bubbling to the front of the laminate which would need to be covered up somehow, and since we are thinking outside of the box in this chapter... I was thinking cork, as you do! I had found some old cork tiles in a charity shop a while back and had been saving them for a rainy day. Cork is a sustainable, natural material with a timeless appeal and I thought it would be an interesting project to demonstrate the use of more unusual materials in your upcycling projects.

SELECT MATERIALS

- Multi-surface primer
- Eggshell paint
- Short pile mini roller & tray
- Small brush
- Tape measure & pencil
- Wood glue
- Flat brush
- Cork tiles
- Cutting board
- Precision craft knife
- Painter's masking tape
- Satin polyurethane topcoat (use satin for a slight sheen to the final finish)

1. Clean your piece down first with degreaser and a kitchen sponge. As this piece was laminate, it was particularly important to remove any dirt or grease because the surface is naturally more difficult for paint to stick to.

2. Next, I removed the handles, and then the doors, with a screwdriver **(a)**. Keep in mind that particle board can disintegrate when messed around too much, so where possible consider leaving cabinet doors or hardware on if appropriate so not to disturb the fixings. Mine had bubbled up around the hinges due to water damage, so I had to remove everything to repair it. To repair damaged laminate, use an epoxy resin filler. (See Chapter 3 for repairing particle board.)

3. With the repairs done, sand the slippery laminated surfaces to give the cabinet some grip or tooth for the paint to grab onto. (See Chapter 3 for sanding.) Be sure to be thorough with this step as sanding is essential before painting laminate. I recommend using an orbital sander for the larger surfaces **(b)** and then hand sanding details such as the legs on this piece.

4. Wipe down with a tack cloth to pick up any dust, then apply a good multi-surface primer suitable for laminate surfaces onto the entire cabinet frame with a mini roller, including the legs. Move on to priming the door and drawer fronts (I used grey primer here). Even though I'd be covering the door and drawer fronts with cork in the next steps, I primed these as well to ensure the cork would adhere properly later **(c)**.

5. Once the primer is completely dry, paint the cabinet with your chosen colour. (See Chapter 3 for painting.) I chose a dark shade of eggshell to create a striking border around my cork panels, but you could definitely play around with more colour here if you wanted to.

6. Paint the legs with a small brush **(d)** and do the same for the door panels and drawers, particularly the edges which will be still be on show once the cork is fitted.

7. Mark out a centre point on your drawer and door fronts using a tape measure and pencil **(e)**. I recommend doing this when the material you are using will not cover the whole area in one piece, as it helps to make everything look symmetrical. For this cabinet, I divided each area to be covered into quarters, but you could also try dividing the area in half depending on your preference.

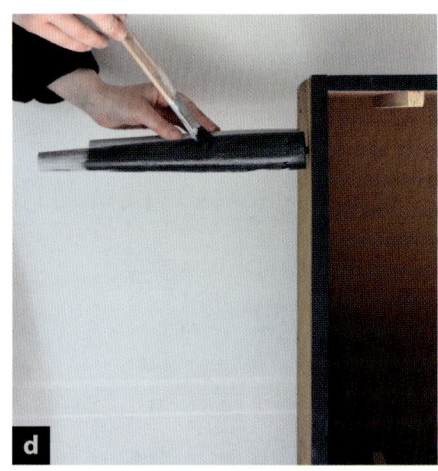

ALTERNATIVE TECHNIQUES

8. Next, I applied wood glue to the first section using a flat brush. Apply enough glue on the surface for the cork to properly adhere to, as shown **(f)**. I am completing the process section by section so that the glue remains wet, and I can still see the lines underneath. This way I am able to keep the cork exactly straight, but this is optional.

9. At this stage there is no need to cut the cork to size. Place a full tile onto the glue where you have marked your centre point, lining it up and pressing the cork down firmly **(g)**. Leave the rest of the cork to overhang any edges. At this stage some glue may seep through to the surface of the cork; in which case you can wipe this away with a damp cloth.

10. Continue to add pieces of cork, gluing as you go and butting each piece up against the other firmly until the whole area is covered. Then proceed to cover the rest of the drawers and doors by repeating Steps 8 and 9 for each.

11. Wait for the glue to completely dry, as this will make the cork easier to cut. Turn each covered surface upside down and place onto a cutting board, then cut away the excess using a really sharp craft knife, pressing the blade against the flat edge of the door or drawer to get a straight line.

12. Once the excess is trimmed and dry, hold your cutting knife at a 45-degree angle and cut around the edges of each piece again, **(h)**. This is to avoid the cork catching or lifting up when in use, and will also neaten up the edge.

123

13. Use a fine-grit sandpaper to sand and smooth down all of the edges **(i)**. Then take your tack cloth to remove any dust that has resettled on the surface ready for sealing.

14. At this stage you may find that the edges of the doors and drawers need a touch-up, so use painter's tape to create a neat line with a detail brush, and once the paint is dry peel the tape away.

15. As cork is a porous material, it will need to be sealed to make it waterproof and practical for daily use. For this I chose a clear polyurethane with a satin sheen and a mini roller. (See Chapter 3 for sealing.) I used a short pile roller to cover the rustic cork surface more effectively **(j)**. Apply three to four coats, fine sanding between each to get a smoother result.

16. Next, I refinished the hardware to add a little colour to this piece. However, feel free to skip this step if not necessary.

17. Add the hinges and handles back on. I used a very small screwdriver (but you could use a bradawl) to make a hole carefully through the back of the cork surface, and then reattach.

TIP

For an ultra-glossy and harder-wearing finish, consider using a resin coating to seal in the cork. This will create a glass-like, crystal-clear finish.

You could easily use the same technique to apply a variety of different materials to the front of your vintage cabinet. Get creative and try out old postcards or book pages, even wood trim arranged in patterns.

ALTERNATIVE TECHNIQUES

SPRAY PAINTING HANDLES

Spray paint is often my go-to paint for revitalising old hardware as it is quick and avoids any thick brush marks, achieving a professional finish. I really loved these vintage 1960s handles in the brass but felt that something was missing from the overall look and I wanted to add some bright colour. A change in the style or colour of handles can really change the feel of an upcycling project, as we see here. You could fully spray the handle if preferred, or try out different colour combinations for a bolder look.

YOU WILL NEED

- Fine sandpaper
- Tack cloth
- Tape measure
- Painter's masking tape
- Clear primer
- Spray paint
- Screwdriver

1. Mark the centre point of the handle using a tape measure, and cover one half with painter's masking tape.

2. Clean and sand down the side of the handle to be painted with fine sandpaper, then wipe over with a tack cloth. Apply clear primer to the exposed half.

3. Once dry, shake the spray paint can according to the manufacturer's instructions, making sure it is properly mixed. Spray each handle at a distance in fine thin coats. As you spray, try to make it one flowing movement from one side to the other, avoiding drips or stop and start marks The trick is to begin spraying before you get to the handle, continuing past the end of it before coming back the other way.

4. Build up the layers gently and slowly in thin passes, letting them dry fully in between coats. Once you achieve full coverage, remove the masking tape to reveal your finished colour-blocked handles **(a)**.

5. Next – the best bit – fix your handles back onto your project using a screwdriver **(b)**. It's amazing how that little flash of colour brings everything together!

ALTERNATIVE TECHNIQUES

project 12
stained glass

before

As a furniture artist I often see glazed units like this one. This cabinet is a really good example, featuring beautiful leaded glass panels – this piece would have once sat on top of a dresser or bookcase which has since been divided into two – because as our style of living has changed, our needs have as well! We don't read as many books, or have so many precious artefacts to display; and our houses have got smaller, so people tended to break larger pieces up to save on space. It's often the dresser tops like this one that become redundant, and I really wanted to show you how to repurpose this into something more useful for the way we live today, turning it into a colourful drinks cabinet. The beautiful hand-cut leaded shapes have inspired me to create a stained glass effect which is going to look amazing lit up. You don't have to use all the techniques you see here on one cabinet, though; even just one change to your glass project could be a big transformation! I've included a few glazed projects in this book because glass tends to get overlooked, and it has so much potential sometimes you just have to look past paint as the only answer!

SELECT MATERIALS

- Painter's masking tape
- Precision craft knife
- Water based primer
- Eggshell paint
- Mini roller & tray
- Small brush
- Glass cleaner
- Lint-free cloth
- Wooden legs x 4
- Tape measure
- Cordless drill & wood drill bit
- Instant grab adhesive
- Coloured vinyl film
- Water mister
- Sharp scissors
- Felt-edged squeegee
- LED lighting kit *optional*

1. First, remove the delicate glass doors with a screwdriver and put them somewhere safe **(a)**. I was really careful here as these doors in particular are made from handmade leaded glass, so if I broke a panel, it would be very hard to replace. Then, remove all the hardware as needed, especially the shelf supports on a project like this, putting them aside for clean-up if necessary.

TIP
The price of vinyl can add up if you want to use a lot of colours on your project. I would recommend buying samples instead, or asking your supplier if they have any off-cuts available. These will come on smaller sheets to save on cost without compromising on style.

127

2. It is quite common for these glazed cabinets to have a backboard, but on this occasion, I felt it looked a little old-fashioned, so I decided to remove it to create a more modern and streamlined look. Look for where this is screwed in; however, if the screws are concealed, use a hammer and brute force to remove the backboard as I had to do here **(b)**!

3. Fill the holes left behind and any other areas that need attention with epoxy resin wood filler. (See Chapter 3 for wood filling.)

4. Prepare the cabinet and glazed doors for priming by cleaning, using degreaser and a kitchen sponge, and sanding everything down. (See Chapter 3 for cleaning and sanding.) I'd recommend hand sanding to avoid any damage to the glass; if using an orbital sander, be extra gentle or use on a low speed, as the vibration can sometimes cause the glass to break.

5. To prevent paint from going on the glass panels, I prefer to mask along the edge inside and out with painter's masking tape, pressing down really firmly and cutting off the excess with a sharp utility blade **(c)**. Alternatively you could try just painting over the glass, using the blade to scrape away the paint once it's dry, but it really depends on the project, and personal preference, as to which method you decide to use.

6. Prime the whole frame and the doors. (See Chapter 3 for priming.) For this type of project, I use a mini roller as much as I can, keeping the coverage quite light on the thinner areas like the edge of the doors to avoid any build-up of paint; and then a detail brush to get into the awkward areas. I also painted the interior of the cabinet and the door frames while these are removed, for a neater finish. I used a white water based primer as I planned to use a light pink eggshell paint for the topcoat. However, consider using an oil based primer if you experience any bleed through; it can be common with a cabinet as old as this for wood tannins to show underneath the paint.

7. Once the primer is dry, repeat the painting process again for the final colour **(d)**. Because I used very pale pink on this piece, I had to do around four coats for proper coverage.

ALTERNATIVE TECHNIQUES

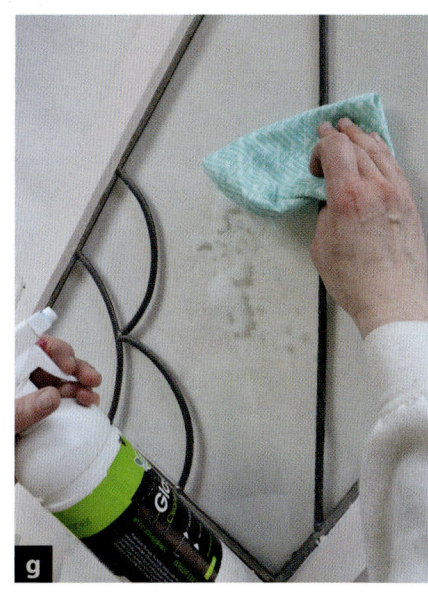

8. When the paint is dry, run a sharp blade gently along the edge of the painter's masking tape where it meets the frame, being careful not to scratch the glass underneath **(e)**. This will create a cleaner line and prevent the paint from peeling away when you come to remove the tape. Once removed carefully, I like to clean up the glass using a smear-free glass cleaner and a lint-free cloth; keep these handy as we will need to clean again in the later steps.

9. To achieve more of a drinks cabinet feel, we will need to raise this off the ground. I found some wooden legs online to complement the curvy shapes in the leaded glass; these are brand new, but you could definitely reuse vintage legs if you wanted to. To fit, I turned the cabinet upside down and, using a tape measure, marked where each leg should go on all four corners so that they were evenly spaced. Then, with a cordless drill I drilled a hole the same size as the screw fitting using a wood drill bit.

10. To add extra strength, I applied instant grab adhesive to attach the legs to the base, then screwed in each leg tightly **(f)**, wiping away any excess glue, and leaving to dry fully before painting to match the cabinet.

11. While the legs are drying, find a clean, dust-free area and place the glass doors on top of a clean flat surface. Then use glass cleaner and a lint-free cloth to clean again **(g)**. This step is crucial when using vinyl, as any dust particles, dirt or fingerprints left on the panes of glass will show up underneath the vinyl covering. (Repeat this process as you apply each piece of vinyl, as dust always seems to appear from nowhere!)

12. Using sharp scissors cut a piece of vinyl roughly the size of the shape you want to cover, keeping the backing on. This doesn't have to be exact but leave an overhang on each side for your fingers to go (I suggest an inch if possible), to avoid fingerprints from holding the vinyl being seen on the other side of the glass. It will also give you more room to play with, making it easier to lay the vinyl down into the right spot first time.

13. Peel away the backing ever so slightly in one corner, then hold up the piece of vinyl, using the other hand to peel away the rest of the backing slowly **(h)**. Do this bit by bit, lightly spraying the reverse of the vinyl as you go with a water mister to weigh it down a little; and keep going until the whole of the vinyl has a light dusting of water with all of the backing now removed. Of course it is good to have a helper for this part, though it is not essential.

129

14. Lightly spray the glass you are applying on to, then work quite quickly, holding the vinyl as taut as possible and keeping your fingers on the very edges. Then lay it down so the section of glass is fully covered. Do this in one motion to avoid any dust particles getting stuck to the back of the vinyl; try to avoid moving it around or peeling it back again once it has hit the glass.

15. Press down on the vinyl slowly, starting from the middle point and working outwards, using your felt-edged squeegee tool to push out any air bubbles **(i)**. If the vinyl doesn't stick flat onto the glass around the very edges, this is quite normal and the edges will flatten as the water evaporates. The main aim at this point is to get it in the right position.

16. Take a precision craft knife and, using the edge of the cabinet as a guide, carefully trim the excess **(j)**. Use a firm and steady hand but be confident and try to use one long smooth motion instead of stopping and starting, as this will ensure a clean cut. Remove the excess vinyl and then smooth down the edges using the squeegee to push out any leftover air bubbles.

17. Continue to fill in each panel, until you are happy with the design – with this piece I wanted to apply vinyl to the sides of the cabinet as well as the doors **(k)**. Then add the hardware back on and reattach the doors.

18. You can leave your project here if you want to. However, I decided it would be nice to make the drinks cabinet light up. To do this I added a standard LED lighting kit which you can purchase from any DIY store **(l)**.

TIP

It is quite common for old glazed cabinets to have wooden shelving but I would suggest getting replacement toughened glass shelves made from your local glazier. This works really well with a drinks cabinet design because light can shine through each layer.

ALTERNATIVE TECHNIQUES

ADD LIGHTING

An optional extra to make any upcycled furniture project really shine as it deserves. LED lighting is easy to install and is the perfect addition to create a high-end look, especially when revitalising glazed cabinets which lend themselves very well to the glitz and glamour. I must say, however, although we are using off the shelf kits, it's always a good idea to get your lighting checked by a qualified electrician.

YOU WILL NEED

- LED lighting kit
- Aluminium LED profile
- Sharp scissors
- Painter's masking tape
- Hacksaw
- Strong contact glue
- Bradawl
- Screwdriver
- Cordless drill & wood drill bit

1. LED lighting kits are easy and safe to use, and the strips supplied can be cut to size to suit the project you are working on. First measure the cabinet on the back edge and cut the LED light strip to the correct length with a pair of scissors. Make sure you cut through the strip correctly according to the manufacturer's instructions.

2. Then measure out the same length of aluminium profile (which comes in two pieces), marking the amount using a piece of painter's masking tape **(a)**.

3. Cut the aluminium profile down to size using a hacksaw, then use a strong contact glue to stick the LED light strip securely inside the aluminium profile **(b)**. Finally, click on the plastic cover; this will ensure that the light strip stays securely in place while looking neat and tidy.

4. With your LED lighting kit, you will find small clips supplied to attach to the cabinet. Mark each one out using a bradawl to pierce a tiny hole into the wood, and then use a screwdriver to screw each clip into the cabinet.

5. Finally, clip the light into place and drill a hole for the power cable to go through **(c)**. Use a cordless drill for this step with a wood drill bit slightly larger in width than the size of the cable, and then thread the cable through the hole, so it can be connected to the mains plug.

chapter 8

refinishing

Every so often you come across a lovely natural wood piece with a beautiful grain and it's nice to have the option not to cover this up if you don't want to. Paint will always be a large part of refinishing and I'm very happy about that, but the projects here will show you how to balance characterful wooden surfaces with a modern update. I was actually surprised when I put this book together quite how much I use restorative techniques on a daily basis to complement the projects I take on as a furniture artist. In the past when I have explained to people what I do for a living there always seemed so much more to the story than just painted furniture. I think 'refinishing' is a good umbrella term to describe not only painting, but equally traditional restorative processes like sanding, stripping, and sealing wood. I love the artistic side of furniture refinishing – the colours, the pattern and design elements – but soon understood that to create the projects I wanted to, I would need to learn so many other different skills. With a variety of techniques in your repertoire you will have many options when considering what to do with a piece of furniture, which is helpful when no two pieces of vintage furniture are ever the same; you can always expect the unexpected! It's likely that you will also achieve longer-lasting, more professional results the more skills you learn; and of course trying out some traditional refinishing techniques can accentuate the original character of a piece, while giving it a fresh update at the same time. So in this chapter, here are some ideas on how to balance both!

project 13

bare naked

before

Every so often you come across something you have never seen before and I was stunned when I first laid eyes on this Victorian pine tallboy which still had all its original brass cup handles. It could have easily been sitting for sale in a high-end antique shop, but this is the beauty of shopping second hand – you never know what you are going to find. I had been working on a social media campaign at the time and had desperately been looking for something classic and quintessentially English that would suit the brand. This chest of drawers was perfect for the job: honest, rustic and incredibly well made; however, the chestnut brown varnish wasn't original and covered up the wood grain. I was confident I would find a gorgeous farmhouse pine patina underneath, and I wanted to show this off to its full potential. Notice also in this project that I don't really repair or alter anything, I am just looking to preserve and enhance what is already there. This technique is both useful and important to know, particularly if you are more into restoration than refinishing or, like me, love a combination of the two.

SELECT MATERIALS

- Disposable gloves
- Paint stripper
- Old paintbrush
- Stripping knife
- Small wire brush
- Fine wire wool
- Methylated spirits
- Degreasing cleaner
- Kitchen sponges
- White wax
- Clear wax
- Wax brush
- Lint-free cloths
- Sanding block *optional*
- Sandpaper
- Tack cloth

1. To get started I removed the antique brass hardware with a screwdriver, taking care to avoid damaging the screw heads and putting everything in a safe place for later.

2. Work in a well-ventilated space and lay down sufficient protection on the floor or surface you are working on, as this method gets messy. Wearing disposable gloves to protect your hands, apply paint stripper to the piece using an old paintbrush; spread an even layer quite liberally on the surface **(a)**. You may start to see a reaction straight away, but at this point I like to add another layer of stripper working it into anywhere that hasn't bubbled up yet. Leave the stripper doing its work for about an hour; this will vary according to the manufacturer's instructions. (See Chapter 3 for stripping.)

3. Once the paint stripper has bubbled up well, use a stripping knife to remove the peeling varnish or paint **(b)**. Use long, gentle strokes in the direction of the grain, being careful not to gouge the wood, and have a container handy to remove the excess from your scraping tool every so often to avoid clogging up the blade. If the old finish is not entirely removed in the first run, apply another layer of stripper and repeat the process as needed.

4. For detailed areas such as edging, use a small wire brush to remove any peeling varnish or paint **(c)**; this will get into the places the stripping knife can't reach. Rub backwards and forwards gently, going with the grain if possible, to remove everything. You can also use a small screwdriver or the edge of a blade very carefully to get into the really tight spots.

   Once this is done, you might be left with a sticky residue on your piece, as paint stripper remains wet for a long time. To remove this, use fine wire wool and methylated spirits, rubbing along the whole surface of the piece. **(d)** This will clean everything up and even out any remaining finish still hanging on despite the early steps; the wire wool will also smooth the wood grain back down.

5. Then clean your piece thoroughly, using degreaser and a kitchen sponge to get rid of all the residue. At this stage I also cleaned the interior of the drawers and the back of the cabinet, getting rid of any dust and build-up of grime, then left the piece to dry out fully overnight.

6. This gave me time to look at cleaning up the handles. I really love the weathered brass patina on these as you can't buy character like this – it would be hard even to recreate it – so I'm keen to keep everything in the original condition; as a result the clean-up process is very gentle. (If you would prefer shiny handles, see Chapter 3 for cleaning hardware.) I didn't want to use anything to strip the old finish away, so I simply rubbed clear wax into each handle using a kitchen sponge, and then used a lint-free cloth to buff each one to a smart brassy shine. This process preserves what is already there but enhances the character.

7. Once your piece has been left overnight and feels completely dry to the touch, you will need to sand the surface a little more, ready to refinish with wax, oil or polyurethane depending on preference **(e)**. I purposely didn't use an orbital sander for this part because I felt it would be too harsh and remove some of the patina I wanted to keep. So instead I gently hand sanded the chest, using a sanding block and fine grit sandpaper, going in the direction of the grain.

8. For sanding intricate details, try folding your sandpaper in half and then refolding when it gets worn to get to the tight spots. Try to avoid using a the wire brush at this stage; sandpaper is a better option for getting the surface smooth for refinishing.

9. Once everything is sanded, wipe down the piece with a tack cloth very lightly to remove all the dust, ready for sealing **(f)**.

10. Next, to seal and protect the wood, I used white wax **(g)**. This is perfect to tone down the orange shades in old pine and creates more of a contemporary feel. It also gives a natural look while intensifying the wood grain, so it's perfect for these drawers, as they have a nice rustic patina. However, you could use clear wax if you would prefer. Apply wax in manageable sections across the cabinet; I like to use a wax brush for the details and a lint-free cloth or sponge for the large flat areas. Rub in a circular motion, pressing the wax well into the grain. You will immediately see that the wood grain is enhanced but gets a little paler in colour. Don't be too worried about the wax looking too white as you apply; it will tone right down as we move through the next steps. (See Chapter 3 for waxing.)

11. Once the wax has been applied it can look a little dull and cloudy; however, at this point we can buff the surface with a lint-free cloth **(h)**. Use circular motions to remove any excess wax sitting on the surface, then repeat the process until you achieve the desired level of sheen. You will find that the white wax will start to fade as you rub it away, leaving a pale washed look to the wood. If you feel the surface looks too white for your preference, try adding clear wax in the same way as before to dilute the colour a little. For unfinished wood like this, I suggest waxing a couple of times, giving some curing time in between to offer good protection, but this is not essential.

12. As a finishing touch, I made sure the reverse of the piece was clean and then waxed the wood with clear wax, helping to preserve it for the future **(i)**. I love the fact that there was some green paint already on here from a previous life so I left this exactly as it was to show some of the past history, (they used to paint stuff in the old days too you know!).

13. Finally – and this is my favourite part – add the hardware back on and suddenly all your hard work will come together. These old handles are showstoppers and really pop against the stripped wood. It is so nice to see this antique piece of furniture (over 100 years old) looking maintained and ready for a new phase of life – what a natural beauty.

project 14
harlequin oak

before

A local vintage dealer had this piece on sale for a really reasonable price, probably because bureaus over the years seem to have lost their relevance in modern homes. The pen and paper have been in steep decline while the laptop remains ever popular. However, I love the idea of a bureau as a space-saving office idea – there's something nostalgic about sitting at a desk like this; and since so many of us now work from home, I snapped this up. It's amazing quality and made from solid oak so little repair work was required, except for the tricky task of stripping back all that dark brown varnish typical of the 1930s. I was really inspired by the shape of the original handles, which gave me the idea to create harlequin shapes across the front; however, you could do stripes or a checkered effect using the same technique. I love the idea of using a classic pattern in a contemporary way, against the natural wood on this lovely tiger oak desk. Geometric patterns are a great way to update an old piece of furniture yet maintain its original character.

SELECT MATERIALS

- Tape measure
- Spirit level
- Pencil & rubber
- Painter's masking tape
- Sharp utility blade
- Clear polyurethane (matt)
- Detail brush
- Metallic acrylic paint
- Kitchen sponge
- Mini foam roller & tray

1. Begin by unscrewing the hardware with pliers. Sometimes the handles can be tricky to pull out so use the back of your pliers to give them a tap if this happens. I remove the base plates carefully using a flat tool such as a stripping knife, making sure I don't damage the wood beneath **(a)**. Keep the original handles and fixings safe as these can be extremely hard to replace if you lose them – trust me, I've been there!

2. The varnish on this bureau was really thick, so I decided to use a carbide scraper to remove it before the sanding process **(b)**; this means that cleaning beforehand isn't necessary. Start by bringing the carbide scraper towards you, while holding the tool flat against the surface of the wood. Go with the grain, pushing downwards on the tool to achieve the best results. Remove as much dark varnish from the surface as possible on all sides.

BETTER THAN NEW

TIP

For a simpler approach, try making a harlequin stencil, using a piece of A4 card folded into quarters. Then draw a straight line across the corner to the size you want and cut across with scissors, leaving an even shape; draw around it to create identical harlequins. This would work well on a flat table top, for example.

3. As I was leaving some natural wood exposed on the finished piece, I sanded the surface fully with an orbital sander and sanding discs; this gave an even and smooth finish to the oak, and left the wood in good condition for painting and sealing later. (See Chapter 3 for sanding.)

4. Next, use medium grit sandpaper to hand sand any details the carbide scraper and sanding couldn't get to, such as feet and trims **(c)**. I used mine folded over and kept refolding in a different place when it became worn, to help get into the tight spots. You could also use a flexible sanding sponge for this step.

5. With a tack cloth, wipe across all surfaces of the desk inside and out to remove any sanding dust.

6. Now work out where you want to place your pattern. I always start by marking a centre point to work from with a tape measure **(d)**.

7. Then, using a spirit level to check your lines are straight, with a pencil join up a vertical line down the centre of your project, and continue to make vertical lines through where each handle sits. I am keeping in mind where the hardware is going to be and making sure my design takes this into account, so that the final piece looks balanced. For example, on this piece I managed to get the harlequin shapes to cover each handle space fairly evenly **(e)**.

8. You can now mark out horizontal lines through each handle as shown, which will provide you with anchor points for your harlequin pattern or whatever pattern you decide. Divide the space in between these lines into relatively equal parts as you see fit, creating a grid of squares, then connect up the harlequin shapes from corner to corner with your pencil and level **(f)**.

REFINISHING

9. Apply painter's masking tape to outline each shape **(g)**. My bureau was quite rustic and had a lot of detailing to navigate around, so I added the tape in sections, which is more time consuming. However, if you have a nice flat surface you can tape up the whole piece in one go if you prefer, using a sharp utility blade to remove the excess tape where it crosses over.

10. Press down the painter's masking tape firmly. If at this point there are any pencil lines on show within the shape you have taped, use a rubber to remove them, before painting over the edges on the inside of your shape with clear polyurethane and a detail brush **(h)**. This seals the tape edge and will prevent any paint bleeding underneath later on. It's genuinely worth taking the time to complete this step because it will save you so much time in the long run and will create a really neat finish.

11. After the polyurethane is completely dry, you can begin painting each section. I like to dilute the acrylic metallic paint first so that it will absorb into the grain of the wood, creating more of a washed effect and allowing the patina of the natural oak to show through from underneath. A 50/50 ratio of paint to water should achieve the right consistency.

12. Dab your sponge into the paint – you will only need a tiny amount as a little goes a long way – then rub into the grain of each harlequin section **(i)**. Once the first layer is dry, repeat this process as desired, depending on how opaque you want the final finish to be. I used two coats of paint to create the look I wanted.

13. Wait until the final layer of paint is just dry to the touch and then slowly remove the painter's masking tape, revealing the final design **(j)**. Doing this just as the acrylic paint has dried prevents any paint peeling away with the tape and keeps your design looking neat and tidy.

141

14. For my project, I then slightly distressed the edge of the drawers with fine grit sandpaper **(k)**. This finished everything off nicely and gave a professional look to the desk.

15. Let the paint dry overnight and then use a rubber to rub away any remaining pencil lines still on show before sealing your work fully. If you have any areas that need touching up due to bleed-through, you can use a detail brush to do this.

16. Using a smooth mini roller, I sealed the paintwork and exposed wood by applying clear polyurethane **(l)**, leaving time in between coats according to the manufacturer's instructions. (See Chapter 3 for sealing.) I would go for a matt polyurethane on this project for a rustic look. It's a good idea to do a small test first on an inconspicuous spot with your chosen topcoat before committing to the final finish.

17. Lastly, clean the original handles – I lightly rubbed all the handles down with fine wire wool to remove any rust. Then wax and buff to a sheen with a lint-free cloth and you are ready to reattach **(m)**.

project 15

fade to black

before

When this art nouveau sideboard turned up I felt as though I had struck gold. It is actually one half of a dresser, which you may have noticed as a running theme throughout this book. This one is an extra-nice example, though, dating from around the 1900s and made from solid mahogany. I loved the hand-carved panels and the beautiful art nouveau handles. The technique I am using is extremely useful if you want to keep the balance between old and contemporary; for me it works really well when you still want to see some original character. I was inspired by the ancient Japanese technique of Shou Sugi Ban, a practice of preserving wood by charring it with fire. Here I have tried to come up with an alternative (and safer) way to achieve a similar effect with paint. This technique is a modern process but with its inspiration set in history; and I always feel that black is a sophisticated colour that goes well with a more traditional look. You can also try this technique in different colours; white, in particular, is great for creating a lime-washed look, and works incredibly well to lighten the warmer tones in darker woods. (For more information on a white-washed look, see Project 2.)

SELECT MATERIALS

- Water mister
- Round blending brush
- Small brush
- Chalk-based paint
- Kitchen sponges
- Lint-free cloths
- Orbital sander & sanding discs
- Sandpaper
- Wax brush
- Clear wax
- Black wax

1. Remove the handles carefully with a screwdriver and put aside for later. These original art nouveau examples were very pretty with a stunning patina, so I didn't need to clean them up too much, but removing them before painting creates a more professional finish at the end of the project.

2. As this was once part of a larger piece of furniture, I was left with some excess wood on the back where the top was once attached, so I decide to remove that. If you need to do this, mark a straight line where you need to cut off the excess piece. Then use a panel saw to cut; for the cleanest cut, don't use too much pressure but let the weight of the saw do the cutting.

TIP

Choose a piece of furniture made from solid wood or a beautiful wood veneer for this technique, as this paint effect relies on using the natural wood grain to your advantage. This is a great way to give an antique piece a contemporary update.

BETTER THAN NEW

3. Remove the previous finish using a carbide scraper **(a)**. You may be asking why, if we are going to paint it anyway? But this is an important step because for this technique we need the grain of the wood to show through from underneath the paint. It will also allow the paint to soak into the surface, creating more of a natural look. That said, it's not essential to remove absolutely everything; some varnish left underneath is not a problem and can add a bit of character and variation to the final finish.

4. For the carved panels, I recommend using a little bit of paint stripper and a small wire brush to remove the dark varnish, as this will allow you to get into all the details on a piece like this more effectively **(b)**. Then follow the rest of the steps for liquid stripping and clean-up detailed in Chapter 3.

5. Once the panels are fully dry, use fine sandpaper and a sanding block to smooth over the surface of the sideboard. You could use an orbital sander and sanding discs if you want to, but it's not necessary to be too thorough with this step, so a light sand is fine. Rub the whole piece down with a tack cloth to remove any sanding dust before painting **(c)**.

6. I recommend working one side at a time for the next part. First, spray the surface very lightly with water, using a water mister; you will only need a minimal amount but the moisture will allow you to spread the paint more easily.

7. With a round blending brush, paint a solid layer of black across the top third; on this piece it worked well to paint across the upper drawer section. The top of the sideboard is where the colour will be most opaque, so you don't need to worry about seeing the wood grain too much as you paint, but keep in mind that we will be fading out the colour towards the base in the following steps. Once you have a strip of paint along the top, spray the bottom of this painted area with a water mister **(d)**.

REFINISHING

8. With the paint now a little wet, blending is a lot easier and we can create a faded effect moving down the piece. Use a kitchen sponge or a lint-free cloth to spread the paint downwards towards the base, as this will give a softer look than a brush **(e)**. Keep spreading out the paint where you feel the sideboard needs it, rubbing into the surface for more of a translucent effect instead of complete coverage.

9. Once the sponge has dried out a little, pass it over any carved areas and details very lightly so that these just pick up a small amount of paint **(f)**; it will help to highlight the features and add more of an authentic aged look, giving variations in tone.

10. At this stage I applied some shading with a small brush **(g)**. I used black paint, focussing on areas of the sideboard where it might naturally hold onto paint, for example around trims, edges and details, and all the places where an old cabinet like this would naturally age.

11. Use your water mister here again if required, and then soften the painted edges using a dabbing motion with a kitchen sponge **(h)**. Hopefully the paint will sit nicely in the crevices, giving a softer and blurry effect.

145

> **TIP**
> Experiment with a drippier paint effect. Mix up a paint wash with water to a 50/50 ratio and pour into a spray bottle; then apply to the piece directly for a slightly grungier look.

12. Next, extend the black paint onto the top and sides of your cabinet if you haven't done so already, continuing to paint the same effect as before. Start with a dark tone at the top, fading down to lighter each time **(i)**.

13. Once this has dried to the touch, use an orbital sander and a fine sanding disc, to take away some of the black paint **(j)**; this seems a little destructive, but it will create a more authentically aged look at the end. Then distress some areas by hand sanding, for example the edges of the drawers or anywhere where there would be natural wear **(k)**.

14. To seal your piece, use a wax brush with clear wax. Cover the whole piece and then use black wax and a kitchen sponge to shade with **(l)**, blending the wood into the painted areas. (See Chapter 3 for waxing.) At this stage you will see the raw wood intensifying in colour, which is really exciting.

15. Buff the surface with a clean lint-free cloth and all that's left to do is pop the handles back on, having revived them using a tiny bit of clear wax and a cloth **(m)**. Then you can sit back and admire your work!

chapter 9

staging and photography

When you finish a beautiful project, I personally think it would be rude not to show it off. Staging and photography are, for me, a way of recording a piece you are proud of and celebrating an accomplishment, whether that's just in a photograph or as you walk past your piece every day feeling really pleased with yourself!

In this chapter I will give you some tips on how to stage, style and photograph your project, to make your home look gorgeous. This process can also be really beneficial if you decide to start selling your work.

When I first began taking photos of my furniture, I soon realised it was mostly about being imaginative and resourceful and often about tricking the eye. I'll let you into a little secret: all of my photographs, even the ones for this book, are created in the tiniest space in my kitchen – I even have to move the fridge at times, much to the disappointment of my husband – yet strangely it all looks very calm and serene in a photograph! Staging is where the magic happens, and I will give you some tips on how to make any space work for you.

The key is to be resourceful, using what you already have where possible. All of the following tricks can be used to style your home or capture a great picture of something to sell, or just to share your pictures or videos on social media afterwards, if that's what you want to do.

STAGING

There's a high possibility that the piece of furniture you have been working on has been sitting unloved in a garage somewhere for years underneath dust and dirt, am I right? Maybe now is the right time for it to shine once again; and staging can highlight features, functionality and charm, making something that was previously unloved look extra special.

I keep a few things in mind when I'm staging a piece. It's nice to set the scene, so a person can imagine your piece of furniture in their own home (an example of this would be staging a bedside table with books and a cuppa); but for me it's also about thinking outside the box to grab attention, perhaps doing something unexpected – for example using quirky props such as giant palm leaves or branches from the garden, or even carrying

a sideboard off to a nearby field to get the perfect shot. I encourage you to get creative and show off your personality.

Here are some of the things you might want to consider when staging and styling furniture. There are no set rules, but these are the things that go through my head – I hope you feel inspired to try some of them.

SETTING THE SCENE

WHAT'S IN THE BACKGROUND

Using a good backdrop gives a piece of furniture an opportunity to stand out and get noticed. For this I prefer a neutral painted wall in either a light colour or a darker shade; the simplicity of it will highlight your piece and really make it pop out from the scene. You can use a wall in your house or try investing in a backdrop support stand if you need one; these can be put up and taken down easily and you can experiment with hanging fabric, paper and even reusable vinyl backdrops. On the opposite end of the scale, go for a maximalist theme; you can take a 'more is more' approach which is all about contrast, for example clashing patterns, so consider any spaces you have in your house that might create a striking background, such as a wallpapered wall.

STAGING AND PHOTOGRAPHY

DON'T FORGET TO LOOK DOWN

Believe it or not flooring matters and I find it can really emphasise a project if you get it right. I use a white piece of lino left over from my bathroom renovations which I roll up and put away when not in use, but consider using different flooring options depending on the style of your piece. Perhaps you have a space in your house with a beautiful flagstone floor or stripped floorboards. If this is not an option, consider using a rug, laminate off-cuts, painted board or even lining paper on the floor to help highlight your project.

LAYER UP THE SCENE

This will add depth and interest. Use this technique when you want to create a softer lifestyle shot. When your project is in the right position, take a look from a distance to see where the blank space is and where extra layers would be beneficial. Think of layering as colour, texture, flooring, accessories, wall art and your backdrop. Try placing something like a rug on the floor in the foreground, then move onto adding interest mid-level, such as a pile of books; you could also try hanging a frame or print above your piece. The key is to enhance the furniture rather than overcrowd the space, so I think keeping some empty space is also important for balance. Whether it's props, or even a pug in my case, getting these layers all in sync will add a sense of balance to your photographs and grab attention.

LESS IS MORE

There are times when keeping it simple is the way to go. If your backdrop is more detailed (like a rustic brick wall); or perhaps you have a patterned wallpaper as your background, or if the piece itself is complex in design (it may be multi-coloured or highly patterned), then I tend to keep the staging classic and simple. Keep in mind that too much going on in a photograph can detract attention from what is important; props might not even be necessary.

PROPS

Always have a good selection of staging props to choose from; sometimes I don't know where I am going with staging until I see the perfect object to inspire me, so this is why I keep my favourite things in a variety of colours, strong shapes and different textures. See the potential in things you own already around the house; I even pop to my mum's house sometimes to 'borrow' her stuff (it all gets returned, I promise). Consider shopping second-hand for vintage pieces – things like blankets, baskets, frames and pottery are some of my favourite items to find at car boots and charity shops.

REIMAGINE, REUSE AND RECYCLE

When choosing second-hand objects, search for interesting shapes and vibrant colours which will jump out at you or vintage pieces that will tell a story, such as my favourite pile of old books. Vintage items often have more character and can really complement old pieces of furniture; buying these saves on cost and is a good way of reusing items rather than buying new. The added bonus of sourcing second-hand props is that you can treat them in a similar way to your furniture projects; think about giving items a refresh with paint if you want to change the colour. I alter dried foliage all the time with spray paint to suit the scene I am capturing; this is a very quick process and allows me to pick out particular colours in my project to maximum effect. I also like to change up objects such as empty frames, glassware and painted stars to suit the mood of a picture. Reusing what you already have and changing the look with paint is a great idea to save on waste when staging, and is something I do all the time.

BRING THE OUTDOORS IN

I find that foliage and branches are like gifts from nature when it comes to furniture or home staging. I am always in my garden looking for stems such as pampas, dried-out bamboo sticks or allium heads and flowers, because these make brilliant props, and are great for your home too. I'd recommend taking a look outside at different times of year, which will provide you with more seasonal foliage, perfect for setting a scene in your photographs and telling a story. If you are lucky enough to be close to some outdoor space, get out there and see what you can find, as the great outdoors is the gift that keeps on giving! You could even try taking a picture of your project outdoors.

MAKE A VIGNETTE

In furniture staging, this is a collection of objects that help to tell a story about your piece. I love to create images like this when I'm staging, getting creative with props and moving in closer to the subject. These shots can really set the whole mood of your project and I find them visually exciting to look at. I'll try not to get too technical here, but generally I like to pick a hero item, a larger object such as a print or mirror; then balance it with smaller objects at the front, maybe in a few different heights. Try not to go for a symmetrical look, instead go for more of a natural placement; personally I like to have the items just touching each other in the frame.

THE PROPS

Here is a list of my favourite staging items. I turn to these time and time again, so I would definitely consider having at least some of them on hand for your next furniture project.

BOOKS

Perhaps my most used prop, these can be stacked up to create different heights, left open to create a homely feel, or to add pops of colour. Keep your eyes peeled for colourful spines, as these look great placed on their side.

FRAMES

Frames are a perfect prop to use for layering. I particularly like an empty frame used behind other objects and they are ideal to fill in bare areas that need a bit of something, but not too much.

PLANTS

Plants – real or fake – are a fantastic way of adding warmth and personality. They look amazing but don't detract too much from the piece and you can play around with them grouped in a collection or dotted around the scene to make more impact.

RUGS

A rug in the foreground of a picture can add a luxurious and homely feel. I tend to stick to neutral tones and natural materials to provide another layer of interesting texture.

THROWS

Throws are so versatile, use them on the floor, hang them from a hook on the wall, fold and place them on a cabinet or drape them over a chair. I have even used a paint-covered dust sheet to set a scene.

VASES

A stylish vase always creates a great photo – you can add flowers and stems for height and interest and experiment with different shapes and sizes. Aside from being practical they can also be a prop in their own right, coming in a mixture of glazes and materials.

BASKETS

A go-to accessory for filling space and adding lived-in charm. You can use as a plant container, hang a collection of baskets on the wall, or place on the floor to anchor your shot.

FLOWERS

Consider using flowers in a few different ways. You can go for dried blooms which can look really effective and can be used over and over again, or alternatively go for fresh flowers to add texture and a cosy feel.

ARTWORK

Artwork is very useful for filling in blank spaces and adding height and colour to a photograph. Look for budget-friendly prints, old birthday cards or postcards.

So now the scene is set. It's time to take some photos!

THE SHOT

Good photographs and videos have genuinely elevated my business over the years; I have been able to create a portfolio of work to show clients, which I share regularly on social media, and photos also provide me with future inspiration for new projects.

Disclaimer: I am no professional photographer, but I really wanted to give you a few straightforward tips for getting some striking furniture shots or videos in case you should ever want to show off your handy work!

A lot of people ask me if you can get by professionally using the camera on a phone, and in all honesty yes, you absolutely can… for most things. However, I would recommend getting a DSLR camera further down the line if you want to see your work in print! A camera like this will take your images in a higher resolution with more clarity, so it's definitely worth considering.

Here's some helpful advice on how to achieve some gorgeous snaps or videos of your furniture projects!

KEEP IT CLEAN

It sounds simple but clean your camera lens; this has caught me out so many times and is an easy fix to achieve crystal-clear photographs. I now do this as standard every time before a shoot.

GET THINGS STRAIGHT

Of course, you can edit your photo afterwards to make small adjustments, but if you get it right in the beginning by lining everything up square, you'll be on the way already to taking a great photo. Try using the grid lines function on your device to help out with this.

MIX UP ANGLES

I like to take a full shot of my piece first and then a mix of close-up, high-up, low-down, from-the-side angles, and even turn my camera upside down to mix things up a bit. Use these shots as an opportunity to show off all of the finer details of your project such as colour and texture.

LEAVE IT OUT

If you work in a small space as I do, then usually I unavoidably end up with unwanted electrical sockets

or the fridge freezer in shot. So make sure to crop away anything unnecessary in the background so that your photograph looks neat and tidy, and your eye is focussed on the project rather than everything around it.

FIND FOCUS

Always check that your camera is in focus before taking a picture. Again, it sounds so simple but it's always the small things that make the most difference. Take a look at the screen before you take the picture and check that everything looks as sharp as it should be.

KEEP IT STEADY

Use a tripod to keep the camera still, meaning you can even step into the photo or film yourself if you want to; this will also prevent blurry photos. If you don't have a tripod, though, think outside the box and utilise what you have. Try propping your phone against a paint can or inside a mug – I do this all the time!

NATURAL LIGHT

I always find that natural light shows off the details of a furniture project so beautifully with little effort, if you can find the right spot. The ideal is to have a natural light source facing your subject, as this will cast an even light onto your piece with no shadows. I have to say, though, sometimes I like the odd shadow in a photo because it creates a mood.

ADD ARTIFICIAL LIGHT

For times when natural light isn't possible, invest in lighting boxes with an adjustable light source or a light ring for your smart phone. These are invaluable for photography because you can control the level of light that you need when natural light is scarce, which gives you more control over your pictures.

DO THE EDIT

I rarely post an unedited photo or video; editing will improve what you already have and put the icing on the cake. Keep in mind, though, that having decent footage in the first place really helps. Try out apps such as capcut, lightroom or inshot for editing your pictures and footage. I particularly like to lighten and sharpen my images or use a healing tool to remove anything unwanted.

resources

A list of my favourite things! I have tried to include everything from paint and wallpaper to my most frequently attended DIY stores. While based in the UK, I have made every effort to include brands that you might be able to find elsewhere. Nevertheless, you can find similar items at any reputable hardware or art store. You can also follow my social media pages, where I give regular updates and advice on the products I use.

PAINT

There are many paint brands on the market but I would say that the following products would be a good place to start. For more information about where and when to use specific paints, see Chapter 2; or it will likely become clear as you work your way through the project ideas in this book.

Daydream Apothecary www.daydreamapothecarypaint.com
A chalk-based paint for creatives. It is a versatile product, perfect for creating a large variety of artistic paint effects such as in Chapter 4. The colours are particularly vibrant and highly pigmented.

Farrow & Ball www.farrow-ball.com
Ideal for flat finishes and readily available in local DIY stores. I like to use Modern Eggshell as this has a quick curing time and a subtle sheen.

Montana Cans www.montana-cans.com
I would recommend Montana Gold for any spray-painted projects such as the hardware in Project 11 (Neon Cork).

Valspar www.valsparpaint.co.uk / www.valspar.com
For smooth finishes, try the water-based Eggshell for wood and metal; in particular the in-store colour-matching service is very useful to colour match chalk-based paint colours where I'm looking for a flatter and more durable finish.

Zinsser www.zinsseruk.com
A great primer in my opinion – typically I use the water-based version of Bulls Eye 123 Primer.

Annie Sloan www.anniesloan.com
Chalk paint ideal for creating distressed or rustic paint effects. I would also highly recommend the wax for sealing chalk paint projects.

Lick www.lick.com

YesColours www.yescolours.com

Graphenstone www.graphenstone.co.uk

Little Greene Paint Company www.littlegreene.com

ART SUPPLIES

Some of these supplies might seem more suited to creating on canvas than furniture, but I have found incorporating art materials into a project – not being limited just by what's available in the DIY store – can really open the mind to a range of alternative ideas.

Arteza www.arteza.co.uk
Has the best and most interesting selection of palette knives and painting tools in all shapes and sizes.

Caran d'Ache www.carandache.com
The creators of very highly pigmented water-soluble art pastels; ideal to draw with and add details to artwork.

Culture Hustle www.culturehustle.com
A creative supplier of quirky and unusual paint supplies including neons, pigments, metallics and iridescent paint effects – very cool and great quality.

Posca www.posca.com
The 'Posca Pen' has its origins in graffiti art back in the 1980s and as a result these are popular with street artists and people who want to create on the go. These handy acrylic pens are ideal for drawing out and adding finer details to artwork.

Derwent www.derwentart.com
Watercolour pencils are useful drawing tools and, being water soluble, help you to create some great artistic effects.

Daler Rowney www.daler-rowney.com
I like to use the System 3 acrylics, which are quick drying and perfect for hand-painted details.

Winsor & Newton www.winsornewton.com

Pebeo https://en.pebeo.com

Golden Artist Colors www.goldenpaints.com

Liquitex www.liquitex.com

PAINTBRUSHES

Two Fussy Blokes www.twofussyblokes.com
Supplier of premium paint rollers available in a range of different textures.

Zibra www.enjoyzibra.com
A wide range of professional paintbrushes, well designed for sealing and creating a smooth-painted finish.

Annie Sloan www.anniesloan.com
The blending brushes are perfect for soft paint effects and creating texture.

Daydream Apothecary www.daydreamapothecarypaint.com

Great for creating painterly brushstrokes with chalk-based paint – in particular I love the flat brushes for abstract work, washes or applying topcoats, for example in Project 8 (Abstract Landscape).

DIY

DIY stores are useful places to find the general tools and materials needed to complete a furniture project. These tend to be UK specific, but you should be able to find equivalents outside of the UK.

B&Q www.diy.com
For general DIY materials and Valspar colour mixing.

Homebase www.homebase.co.uk
Alongside DIY products, Homebase typically stocks a good range of Farrow & Ball paint and other reputable paint brands.

Screwfix www.screwfix.com
Reasonably priced for tools, accessories and hardware products.

Sheet Plastics www.sheetplastics.co.uk
Stocks a good range of acrylic products, which you can have cut to your desired specifications. I like to use acrylic mirrored panels as featured in Project 10 (Blue Mirror).

Abode Window Films www.abodewindowfilms.co.uk
This is a business local to me, but you can find a range of coloured and decorative window films for delivery on this website, as in Project 12 (Stained Glass).

UK Glass Centre www.ukglasscentre.co.uk
As in Project 10 (Blue Mirror), I used reeded glass to replace the old panels. You can get reeded glass cut to size by entering your required dimensions online. Or find a local glazier in your area.

POLYURETHANE & SEALING

I would highly recommend the brands below when sealing your furniture projects but find more information on the different types of products and when you may use them in Chapter 2.

Osmo www.osmouk.com

Polyvine www.polyvine.com

General Finishes www.generalfinishes.com

WALLPAPER

Anaglypta www.anaglypta.co.uk
As in Project 6 (Mint Geometric); Anaglypta has an archive of classic designs dating from 1887 right up to present day in a range of different textured patterns, from floral to geometric.

Lust Home www.lusthome.com
I have used this exciting wallpaper brand in Project 4 (Retro Memphis) and Project 5 (Leopard Love); as you can see, the designs are bright and bold and the unique designs always make me smile!

Wallpaper Direct www.wallpaperdirect.com
Here you will find both designer and budget wallpaper brands, with something to suit all tastes. They offer a good wallpaper sample service. Try searching for products by colour or design which is a great way to find inspiration for a new project.

TOOLS & MATERIALS

I have listed just a few of my favourite brands here. Hopefully this will get you started, but there are of course many other options.

Bahco www.bahco.com
A Swedish brand with a big selection of hand tools, and the one I couldn't live without – the carbide scraper.

DEWALT www.dewalt.co.uk
Maker of high-quality power tools. Typically I find Dewalt tools are longer lasting and I've become really attached to my cordless drill.

Festool www.festool.co.uk
A top-of-the-game German brand and maker of many high-performance power tools. I bought an orbital sander which I use for pretty much every project. Not cheap, but a wise investment!

Ryobi https://uk.ryobitools.eu
A great affordable power tool brand for beginners; Ryobi should do the job really well even if your budget is tight.

ProDec www.prodec.uk.com
My favourite sandpaper, and this company also make the tack cloths I use throughout the book. They are so handy.

A BIG THANKS TO...

The inventor of pizza, for providing a quick and convenient dinner for the kids each evening.

Guy, for cooking the pizza, his furniture-lifting strength, and always being there for us all.

A well-known soft-drinks company for the low-calorie caffeine highs.

Mum, for her good taste and style, and for teaching me to dream (some might describe it as the ability to be unrealistically positive).

Dad, for his excellent DIY skills and the determination to succeed.

Gran, for making the most of every day, and inspiring me never to quit.

Bailey, Orla and Eden, for being long suffering! I hope that when you read this, you'll feel proud, like I am of you.

My rescue pug Leo... except he rescued me.

My publisher for being patient and challenging me to produce this book. I like to think that good things come to those who wait!

And finally, I'd like to thank myself... for being hard working and mad enough to give this a go!

I love you all, very much, especially pizza!

chloe x